# a working approach to the
# ART ELEMENTS
# and PRINCIPLES
# of ORGANIZATION

**ben cunningham**

**Kendall Hunt**
publishing company

**Book cover credit:** Jean-Luc S. Gallic, "Homage to Helen", data bent image, 2011

"Homage to Helen" was created through the process of "data-bending," which is to alter the code within a digital file. I converted a high-resolution image of a painting by the abstract expressionist painter Helen Frankenthaler into a sound file. After editing this sound file with miscellaneous effects, I am able to convert the file back into an image and what I am left with is a distorted mash of pixels based from the source image data. By removing my visual connection to the piece during the editing process, I facilitate the removal of the artist intention from the creation of an individual work, much like Frankenthaler's painting process of pouring watered down acrylics onto her canvases.

I would like to thank Jean-Luc for allowing me to use his artwork. He is what every teacher hopes will walk into his classroom. I had the pleasure of teaching him 2D, 3D, and Drawing I, and Life Drawing. I expect great things from this gentleman of talent and intelligence.

ben cunningham

**Kendall Hunt**
publishing company

www.kendallhunt.com
*Send all inquiries to:*
4050 Westmark Drive
Dubuque, IA 52004-1840

**I would like to dedicate this book to my sisters:**

*To Debbie, for being my teacher and educator*
*To Chrissy, for being my health and nutritional guide*
*To Joni, for being my compass of truth*

# CONTENTS

# PREFACE

In art, studying fundamental theories and practice can be overwhelming, but doing so is pertinent to anyone interested in the arts. It is the start of a lifelong endeavor full of rewards and revelations. You will not find another area of study that can expand to as profound a depth as you are willing to engage with it.

My objective is to present a comprehensive, synthesized, and simplified art and design textbook, one that merges multiple perspectives of art elements and principles of organization into a single voice for a contemporary art and design classroom.

Foundation courses often are taught by rotating faculty who for the most part would rather be teaching their specialized area of expertise. My intent is to help clarify and unify the instruction of two-dimensional design foundation courses by providing a resource for effectively presenting novice students with a comprehensive platform to scaffold their education.

This book is a synthesis of my studio art experiences, formal training, and desire to prepare my students—as well as possible—to thrive emotionally and financially as contributing members of society, while following their life's passion: making art. It is broken down into a simple, concise, and understandable format in which the students actively participate in the learning process, develop an understanding of art and design foundations, and create a collection of personally relevant images to exemplify the concepts presented.

It has been my experience that most art students are visual, kinetic, experiential learners, who learn best when their hands are busy and their brains are engaged in problem-solving subject matter they find interesting and relevant. This book is not intended to be an art history book, full of images that I find interesting and explain to the viewer, but instead an interactive textbook that the student creates in conjunction with an instructor.

The first section of this textbook focuses on explaining the visual structure of the picture plane. Configured to mimic the creative process, the second section focuses on the introduction and explanation of the individual principles of organization through which the elements are employed: harmony (repetition and rhythm), variety (anomaly, elaboration and contrast), balance (symmetrical, almost asymmetrical, asymmetrical, radial, and crystallographic), focal point/emphasis/dominance, proportion/scale, movement, and economy. The third section of this textbook introduces and explains the physical characteristics and emotional qualities of the individual elements of design (line, shape, texture, value, and color), concluding, in the fourth section, with an overview of space.

Chronologically, each chapter builds upon the information contained in the preceding chapter. The chapters are arranged so that art and design vocabulary and concepts are introduced and then applied by readers as they actively search for relevant visual images. It cumulates with challenging assignments designed to develop technical skill sets that I have deemed as "pertinent attributes our students will need to be competitive in the job market" and rubrics to appraise the students' comprehension and understanding of fundamental art and design theories.

*ben cunningham*

# SECTION 1

## Structurally Understanding The Picture Plane

# ART COMPONENTS

## THREE COMPONENTS OF ART

First, a work of art can be distilled down to an *idea or concept*. This is the part of your design process where you develop the intent of what you want to accomplish. The parts of the concept are idea, research, and editing. Second, an artist needs to decide what *form* or from which *materials* the artwork will be created. This usually is decided through rough and refined thumbnail sketches and material exploration. Finally, an artist needs to decide if her idea and materials work well together. This is referred to as *contextual integration*. This is where you verify if your form meets the expectation of your concept. Ideally, these components work in unison to express the artist's intent.

The creative process is rather fluid. Historically, we are led to believe that artists first come up with an "idea" or subject. Secondly, they determine the materials to be used or "the form." Finally, an artist must decide "how" the activity will manifest. It appears so easy when you explain the process with words. Realistically, as just stated, this sequence quite often is not congruent with the creative process. Often, an artist will just be working in the studio and discover his intent through a dialogue with materials. Whatever the creative process, the strongest works of art depict a fundamental relationship between the artist's idea and materials used. Every work of art can be critiqued or developed through the exploration of its idea, its materials, and the relationship between its idea and materials.

Historically, ideas concerned persons, objects, themes, and configurations of the art elements. Simply stated, it is the starting point. Form is the total manipulation of the elements, line, shape, texture, color, and value to construct an artwork. Finally, content refers to the total message, or intent of the work, as well as the interpretation by the viewer.

An idea can be a person, thing or, as in nonobjective works, the subject is the idea behind the form of the work or process, and is accessible only to those who are versed in formal visual language.

Form is the overall manipulation of the materials used, brought into a meaningful arrangement based on the principles of design. The material and their arrangement have the most important and direct relationship to the artist's intent.

An artist's goal is that the ideas and materials come together into a conceptual integration or organic relationship. An organic relationship is when all the parts of the artwork are interdependent.

## MEDIA AND TECHNIQUES

Media and techniques change so quickly that it almost feels futile to mention them. Trying to learn every new software program introduced or mastering every medium can become an endless task. An individual is better off aligning her skills with her artistic goal.

In studio practice, an artist considers the effect of the media and development of a skill set to execute her ideas. Exploring media, technical skills and truly understanding their expressive capability takes a lifetime of devotion. More importantly, one should develop, simplify, and focus her ideas and explore the expressive language inherent in the medium and its usage.

Art is the physical manifestation of an idea or emotion. Two-dimensional forms are created using line, shape, texture, value, and color. The building blocks of three-dimensional forms are line, plane, volume, mass, space, texture, and color. With time-based art, duration, tempo, intensity, scope, setting, and chronology are combined to create time-based art forms.

The relationship of the elements and the principles of organization are so vital to creating a successful work of art that the remaining chapters of this book are dedicated to introducing and exploring the picture plane, principles, and elements of design.

A completed work of art has three components: idea, materials, and conceptual integration. These components change according to the degree of emphasis put on them. Their interdependence is so great that none should be neglected or given exclusive attention. The whole work of art should be more important than any one of its components.

# THE PICTURE PLANE

The picture plane is defined by the overall size and shape of the edges of the paper, canvas, computer screen, or the margins defined within these edges. This outermost limit should be determined prior to starting an artwork and complement it compositionally. Conceptually, this is no different from determining if your printer should feed the paper in a portrait or landscape orientation.

A two-dimensional artist manipulates forms or elements to visually rest in front of or behind the picture plane. The picture plane is the surface of the paper upon which the design is created. It defines the outermost boundary of a two-dimensional piece or artwork, also known as the picture frame. A three-dimensional artwork's spatial limits are defined by its outermost contour of the form. This concept defines the difference between two- and three-dimensional artwork. Three-dimensional artwork has height, width, and depth. Two-dimensional artwork only employs height and width. In two-dimensional art, all of the picture frame should contribute to the unity of the piece.

## Framal Reference

Within the picture plane is the framal reference. It is the boundary in which the elements exist. It marks the outer limits of a design and defines an area within which the figure (positive elements) and ground (space not occupied by an element) need to exist in unison. Both positive and negative space contribute equally to the overall success of the composition. The framal reference, if it exists, inherently becomes an integral part of the design and its contribution to the overall success of the artwork should not be overlooked.

Composition can be defined as "the combination of multiple parts into a unified whole." In a well-composed design, line, shape, texture, value, and color work together as a team. One element becomes dominant and another element becomes subordinate. A dialogue is created between positive and negative shapes, and opposing forces add vitality rather than creating confusion. Through composition, we can create order, emphasize critical information, and evoke an emotional state.

Art does not just happen. It is a unified whole of similarity and contrasts, created by the art elements line, shape, texture, value, and color, as arranged by the principles of organization harmony, variety, balance, proportion, dominance, movement, and economy, to create a space in which critical information intended to evoke a dialogue is presented.

## Two-Dimensional Art Making Sequence

As stated previously, my intent in writing this textbook is to help artists, as well as neophytes, gain a better understanding of the creative process. To help explain this, I have described the creative process sequentially.

1. An artist selects a picture plane.
2. He has his tools and materials and with them begins to create elements on the surface of the picture plane.

3. Spatial suggestions appear that may conform to his original conception. Otherwise, the process of adjustment begins.
4. The adjustment continues as harmony and variety are applied to achieve balance, proportion, dominance, movement, and economy.
5. As the development continues, the artist depends on his intellect, emotions, instincts, and training. To be successful, the artwork's form has unity and all of the art elements belong and work together.

## Unity

As mentioned, the goal of any artwork is unity. For the artist, unity is the result of selecting the appropriate devices specific to the medium and properly employing certain principles to relate them. In art, an understanding of the principles of organization is indispensable. Through the study of principles of organization, one develops an intellectual understanding that can, through persistent practice, become instinctive.

## Art Elements

The art elements line, shape, value, texture, and color on which form is based rarely exist by themselves. More often, they join forces in the total work. Their individual contributions can be studied separately, but in the development of an artwork, the ways in which they relate to each other must always be considered. Each element makes an individual contribution, and has an intrinsic appeal. Through form, all the art elements need to be considered both individually and collectively.

## UNITY

Unity is the presentation of an integrated image. It is perhaps the only unavoidable rule found in art. A unified artwork starts with a theme that is taken through a number of variations. Thematic material is then woven through the content of the work harmonizing its sections. For the artist or designer, unity results from the selection of appropriate media to be used, the proper use of the tools specific to the medium, and the applicable implementation of specific principles. Through the study of elements and principles of organization, one develops an intellectual understanding that eventually becomes instinctive. An understanding of the elements and principles of visual organization is indispensable.

Unity of design is planned and controlled by an artist. Sometimes, it stems naturally from the elements chosen. But more often it reflects the skill of the designer in creating a unified pattern from varied elements.

An important aspect of visual unity is that the whole must predominate over the parts; you must first see the whole pattern before you notice the individual elements. Each item may have meaning and certainly add to the total effect, but if the viewer sees merely a collection of bits and pieces, then visual unity does not exist.

Artists and designers are visual communicators who arrange the elements of design with a plan. The elements being used need to be controlled and integrated. Artists manage this by discovering and deciding on an appropriate balance of harmony and variety and the application of balance, proportion, dominance, movement, and economy. Together, these guiding principles create space. The sum total, assuming the artist's plan is successful, equals unity.

The mind instinctively tries to create order out of chaos. A designer must provide some visual clues for the viewer to find some coherent pattern or unity. Visual ordering adds harmony to the human visual experience, which would otherwise be confusing. Simply presenting a single theme or idea does not guarantee a unified visual composition. When such a pattern cannot be found, chances are the viewer will simply ignore the image.

# GESTALT PROPERTIES AND PRINCIPLES OF GROUPING

## GESTALT PROPERTIES AND PRINCIPLES OF GROUPING

The main principle behind Gestalt psychology maintains that the human eye sees objects in their entirety before perceiving their individual parts.

Max Wertheimer, along with Kurt Koffka and Wolfgang Köhler, were the three founders of Gestalt psychology. Other important Gestalt theorists are Cristian von Ehrenfels, David Hume, Johann Wolfgang von Goethe, Immanuel Kant, David Hartley, and Ernst Mach.

The study of Gestalt theory sought to define and determine the way objects were perceived. It is based on the question of how we perceive two-dimensional objects. Do we see the figure on the ground of a picture plane or do we see the background that is defining the figure? In design terms, this concept can be described as positive and negative space. The figure or the "positive" is the art element placed upon the background or the "negative space." Understanding this concept will enable you to better grasp the insight of Kurt Koffka when he stated, *"The whole is other than the sum of the parts."* Gestalt theory allows for the breakup of elements from the whole situation into what it really is.

Gestalt theory itself is rather lengthy and complex, dealing in various levels of abstraction and generalization. Gestalt psychologist research is still influencing and making major contributions to the field of art and design. Oddly enough, none of the founders were artists or designers. Until this day, psychologists and not artists perform most of the new knowledge generated and published.

## GESTALT PROPERTIES

The four key principles of Gestalt Systems are: Emergence, Reification, Multistability, and Invariance.

### Emergence

© shymko-svitlana, 2014. Used under license with Shuttertock, Inc.

Emergence is the process of complex pattern formation from simpler rules. It is demonstrated by the process of perception involved in recognizing a dog in the picture above. We see a Dalmatian dog as a whole, staring back at the viewer. The dog is not recognized by first identifying its parts (feet, ears, nose, tail, etc.), and then inferring the dog from those component parts. Instead, the dog is perceived as a whole, all at once. However, this is a description of what occurs in vision and not an explanation how the image of a dog emerges.

In this example, if you relax your gaze and continue to stare at the image, a dog will "emerge" from the complex shapes on the picture plane.

## Reification

© zubarevid, 2014. Used under license with Shutterstock, Inc.

Reification is when our brain "conceives" or "produces" an image that contains more details or spatial information than is physically present in the image.

In this example, we perceive a white square in the middle with a black plus sign floating between the viewer and the black circles. After a few more minutes staring at the image, our brain will unite the four individual squares into one larger square and produce edges that do not physically exist between the squares.

## Multistability

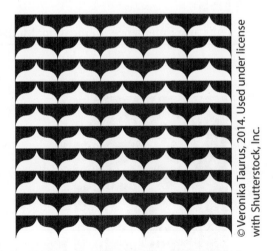

© Veronika Taurus, 2014. Used under license with Shutterstock, Inc.

Multistability is when our brain's perception of the positive space and the negative space flip back and forth between two or more alternative interpretations.

In the multistablity example above, the viewer initially will focus on the white shapes arranged horizontally and pointing upward. After a few minutes, the design will shift from the white shapes to the black shapes pointing downward. The viewer either perceives the white or the black shapes, but not simultaneously. The essence of multistability is that the image is in a constant state of variation. Again, Gestalt does not explain how images appear multistable, only that they do.

## Invariance

© Mila Atkovska, 2014. Used under license with Shutterstock, Inc.

Invariance is the property of perception whereby simple geometrical objects are recognized independent of rotation, translation, and scale—as well as several other variations such as elastic deformations, different lighting, and different component features. Invariance also describes our brain's ability to recognize an object even though we might be experiencing it from a different or unfamiliar angle or perspective. Our perception is not altered even though the image is varied.

In the example presented above, the viewer recognizes the image of a dog even though it is only partially presented.

Emergence, reification, multistability, and invariance can exist individually or in unison with each other to contribute different aspects to a single unified design.

# GESTALT PRINCIPLES AND APPLICATION IN ART AND DESIGN

The fundamental principle of Gestalt perception is the Law of Prägnanz (in the German language, pithiness) that states that we tend to order our experience in a manner that is constant, orderly, symmetric, and simple. These are the same goals that an artist or designer pursues, that of a unified design.

While creating a composition, artists explore and utilize Gestalt principles to analyze their compositions. According to the Law of Prägnanz, visual information is understood holistically before it is examined separately. Applying this theory to composition helps artists create a unified composition for viewers.

When presented with a collection of separate visual units, we immediately try to create order and make connections. This happens because the human mind can only manage a limited amount of information. Our brains are innately programmed to organize material and try to make sense of it. Grouping is one of the first steps in this process. We generally group visual units by location, orientation, shape, and color. For this reason, artworks that are composed of elements that are unrelated in size, style, orientation, and color will appear chaotic and unresolved.

It is vital that artists and designers understand that the individual elements and the composition in which they exist are important both separately and together. They must understand how Gestalt Principles of Grouping influence design.

## Unity in Design

Unity in design is a concept that is heavily influenced and founded in Gestalt theories of visual perception and psychology, specifically those dealing with how the human brain organizes visual information into categories or groups. Gestalt psychologists research design principles which are based on the various relationships governing human perception.

Unity describes the relationship between the individual parts and the whole of a composition: the aspects of a given design that are necessary to tie the composition together (harmony), to give it a sense of wholeness, or to break it apart and give it a sense of differentiation (variety).

In the following section, we will focus on individual Gestalt Laws of Grouping, how they can be used to create successful designs, and how they influence the manner in which a viewer engages with a composition.

The remainder of this chapter will explore eight Gestalt Laws of Grouping: Proximity, Similarity, Closure, Symmetry, Common Fate, Continuity, Good Gestalt, and Past Experience.

## Eight Gestalt Laws of Grouping

For designers and artists, these laws are extremely important because they provide an understanding of how the human brain processes visual information. Artists and designers have assimilated Gestalt principles to unify their artworks. Principles that have been researched and tested have proven to be valuable tools to create successful compositions.

These eight laws of perceptual organization allow us to represent objects from the real world in a two-dimensional composition. They explain how a viewer is able to take a group of seemingly disparate shapes in a design and organize them into something recognizable. An understanding of these eight laws will help you make decisions on how to arrange the individual elements of your design, and predict how they will be perceived.

### 1. Law of Proximity

© Artishok, 2014. Used under license with Shutterstock, Inc.

The underlying concept behind the law of proximity is grouping. Proximity states that independent visual elements, which are arranged close to one another, will be visually grouped together. Even if the elements of a design are not similar in shape, they may be seen as belonging together if they are close to each other in the composition.

Proximity is the simplest way to achieve unity. Without proximity, the artist must put greater stress on other methods to unify an image. It is because of the law of proximity that we are able to read this sentence. The letters that are close to one another become words on the page.

In design, the distance between visual elements is vital to the composition becoming unified. Placing the elements within close proximity helps ensure a sense of unity. Careful use of proximity can create visual tension and add energy to the design. As an artist moves shapes around, she discovers how the mind fills in missing information and determines at what point they begin to "visually" join. With the correct spacing, unrelated elements, shapes, or images may be given a harmonious relationship as they participate in an "implied" grouping. The curved lines of the image above become a group because of proximity to one another.

In the example that illustrates the law of proximity, there are 20 lines, but we perceive the collection of lines in groups. Specifically, we perceive there are five groups of lines.

## 2. Law of Similarity

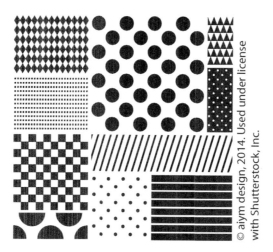

The law of similarity is also based on the concept of grouping. It states that items sharing visual characteristics such as shading, shape, size, color, texture, value, orientation or other qualities will be grouped together by the brain, and a significant relationship between the items will be formed. In addition, items in close proximity to, or aligned with one another, tend to be grouped in a similar way.

The law of similarity states that similar visual elements appear to be grouped together. Elements of a design that look alike are organized into a group. So cones are visually grouped together with other cones, and circles are visually grouped together with other circles, and squares are visually grouped together with other squares. The law of similarity applies to color, size, orientation, texture, and so on.

In the above depiction of similarity, our brain groups the individual squares, circles, triangles, diamonds, and lines together to form the 10 separate rectangles. Our perception of rectangles is due to the law of similarity.

## 3. Law of Closure

The principle of closure refers to the mind's tendency to see complete figures or forms, even if a picture is incomplete, partially hidden by other objects, or if part of the information needed to make a complete picture in our minds is missing. Closure is the idea that the brain tends to fill in missing information when it perceives an object is missing some of its pieces. One reason the mind completes a regular figure not visually depicted is because we are more comfortable with the familiar than with new stimuli. For example, we perceive the image of a panda bear even though the shapes are not connected. If the law of closure did not exist, the image would depict an assortment of different shapes; but with the law of closure, we perceptually combine the new shapes into a familiar entity, a panda bear.

Closure is used extensively in art. It is not so much the quantity, but rather the quality of the information that lets you read an image. A clever artist leaves some things for the viewers to bring to the art. Doing so mentally involves the viewer with your composition. This happens because the human brain wants to simplify and rationalize.

In art, objects are often deconstructed into smaller parts, and when some of these parts go missing, the brain compensates and adds information to replace it. Closure works best with a simple geometric shape, because you need only a few clues to remind you of the shape. More complex objects require more careful consideration as to what can and cannot be removed.

Closure states that individuals perceive grouped together lines, shapes, letters, pictures, and so on as a whole, even though they are incomplete. We tend to ignore gaps and complete contour lines. Closure is the reason we can also make negative areas become specific identifiable forms.

## 4. Law of Symmetry

© AKIllustration, 2014. Used under license with Shutterstock, Inc.

Basically, the law of symmetry states that our mind will perceive a center point and join together two physically unconnected symmetrical elements into a coherent symmetrical shape. The more similar the symmetrical objects are, the greater the opportunity that they will be combined into a symmetrical object. For most humans, a symmetrical type of balance is comfortable, familiar, and a sought after state. In the law of symmetry example above, we tend to observe the three pairs of symmetrical branch-like shapes rather than six individual branches.

In art, a symmetrical balance is also known as "formal" or "mirror" balance. It is perceived as lifeless, consistent, stable, and at times boring. Most architecture is symmetrically balanced so that it is perceived as being structurally sound, coherent, unified, and stable.

## 5. Law of Common Fate

The law of common fate implies the grouping together of objects that have the same trend of motion and are therefore on the same path. The path our eyes will follow is the path of least resistance and we perceive the arranged individual objects as lines. In the example above, the rectangles in the design feel like they are grouped together because of their orientation, their visual diagonal motion, and the perception of paths on which the elements are traveling.

In design, the law of common fate is basically referring to visual directional movements within a design or layout. We give more attention to anything that breaks from a sequence. This phenomenon is what causes us to visualize a cylinder and a circular plane intersecting in the image above.

We perceive items or objects moving (or appearing to move) in the same direction as a group, more so than elements that are stationary or appear to be moving in different directions. Those related items are sharing a "common fate."

Motion attracts attention. Having it in your design will attract a viewer's attention more than a static design. Take a moment and think about your favorite websites. Chances are that they used Flash or J-query to animate the images on the screen. We pay more attention to moving things and even more attention to things moving toward us.

## 6. Law of Good Gestalt/Law of Prägnanz

The law of good Gestalt explains that elements, if they form a pattern that is simple, orderly, balanced, unified, coherent, regular, and so on as possible, will tend to be grouped together.

The human mind will gravitate to a state in which there is order and simplicity and avoid complexity and unfamiliarity. Eliminating extraneous stimuli helps the mind create meaning. The law of good Gestalt focuses on the idea of conciseness, which is what all of Gestalt theory is based on. This law has also been called the law of Prägnanz. Prägnanz is a German word that directly translates to mean "pithiness" and implies the ideas of salience, conciseness, and orderliness.

The human mind wants to simplify and organize complexity. This law explains why the image above is simplified down to being perceived as a plus sign.

## 7. Law of Good Continuation

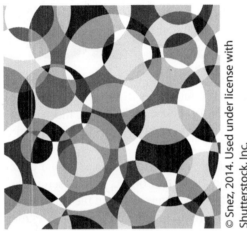

The law of good continuation is a subtler device than proximity or repetition, which are fairly obvious. The law of good continuation states that a series of visual elements connected in a straight or curved line is seen as belonging together. A series of forms lined up in a path will be visually grouped together, even if that path is interrupted by another form. In cases where there is an intersection between objects, individuals tend to perceive the two objects as two single uninterrupted entities. Stimuli remain distinct even with overlap. The law also states that a viewer will follow the path of least resistance or follow the smoothest path.

The law of continuation explains why a viewer is compelled to move smoothly from one object and continue to another. A major component of the law of continuation is that viewers will tend to perceive each object as a single uninterrupted entity and tend to organize lines or curves that follow an established direction (the path of least resistance) over those defined by sharp and abrupt changes in direction. We are less likely to group elements with sharp abrupt directional changes as being one object.

In art and design, the law of continuation describes a device for directing the viewer's attention while he looks at a composition. It is based on the idea that once you start looking in a particular direction, you will continue until you see something significant. Continuation is a type of closure, a grouping of disconnected items held together by the viewer's visual momentum. Since we are taught to read left to right in our culture, this feature is directly built into typography. Once you start reading a sentence, you will continue across a gap to the next word.

As a designer, you will certainly be using this technique in the form of grids, which facilitate good continuation. This basically puts related elements on the same vertical, horizontal, or diagonal line. Rivers, roads, railroad tracks, rows of trees, or telephone poles are informal path devices that artists have used to lead viewers to particular places in their compositions. Like paths, lines of perspective can also be used to direct a viewer's attention to a focal point within a composition.

## 8. Law of Past Experience

The law of past experience states that visual elements are more likely to form a group if that group of elements appears historically associated, familiar, or meaningful to the viewer. If two objects tend to be observed within close proximity, or small temporal intervals, the objects are more likely to be perceived together. In the example above, shapes are arranged in such a way that they resemble the form of a house; then those shapes are seen as a group.

## Conclusion

As shapes are moved around, one should explore the relationship of their placement—the negative interval. Discover how the mind fills in missing information. Determine at what point they begin to "visually" join. With the correct spacing, unrelated elements, shapes, or images may be given a harmonious relationship as they participate in an "implied" grouping.

# ASSIGNMENT 1.1

Find and photocopy two examples for each of the eight Gestalt concepts presented. Paste them into your sketchbook and label them appropriately.

# VISUAL LINKING

In studying Gestalt Laws of Grouping, we explored the relationship of shapes by moving them around. We learned how to create successful compositions; investigated how the human mind perceives, processes, and discovers implied relationships; and how at times, our brain completes the visual arrangements by filling in the missing information. With the Laws of Gestalt, we explored the picture plane horizontally, vertically, and diagonally. In this section, we will explain how visual linking concepts can be used to expand the picture plane's depth of field.

Visual linking picks up where we stopped with Gestalt, but adds physicality to the mix, in what is known as shared space. Shared space is the depth of field that the shapes physically occupy. It is a cohesive device used to help unify a composition by bringing the elements close together. At times, these shapes may physically touch one another. Together, the laws of groupings and visual linking define space on the two-dimensional picture plane.

## TYPES OF VISUAL LINKING

The types of visual linking we will learn about in this chapter are: Connections, Overlapping, Transparency, Interpenetration, and Extensions.

### Connections (Shared Edges)

When shapes share complete sides in common or any form of surface contact, they are activating connections. With connections, the shapes are considered to be sharing the same spatial plane (or depth of field). Connections can only define and suggest a limited depth of field, which is accomplished by manipulating the art elements of design (line, shape, texture, value, and color). When used alone, connections tend to produce compositions that are flat, shallow, and at times, visually confusing.

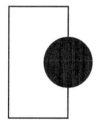  

### Overlapping

As the name suggests, it is the actual "overlapping" of two or more shapes. When one shape blocks or obscures another, these shapes share an area in common, making their relationship more complex than simply sharing a common edge. If the color, texture, value, and so on of the shapes and overlapped area are similar, the shared area can actually unite the two shapes and the new arrangement will define space, albeit a shallow depth of field.

Overlapping does not always result in a shallow depth of field. Through skillful manipulation and an understanding of the art elements, an artist can create as shallow or as expansive a depth of field as desired.

## Transparency

Transparency is similar to overlapping, but with the added ability to see one shape through another. With transparency, the shared area immediately unifies the two shapes, the shared area, and any depth of field that exists between them. This compositional unifying technique activates shallow space, but with enough creativity and problem-solving, an artist can activate as much of a depth of field as her artistic skill level permits.

## Interpenetration

Interpenetration is when at least two shapes appear to be penetrating one another. Their point of intersection suggests and identifies a common depth of field within the two-dimensional picture frame and unifies them visually. Interpenetration can be used to develop and define a shallow or deep depth of field.

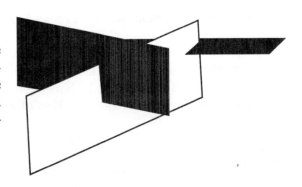

## Extensions

This concept does not rely on shared edges, overlapping shapes, transparency, or interpenetration concepts to relate or integrate forms into a composition, nor is it dependent on the close proximity of forms to develop a sense of unity. Instead, the concept integrates new forms into different and distant areas of the composition and creates space by utilizing a visual alignment system of implied edges, lines, and shapes. Designers and artists use extensions as a subtle means, often in conjunction with grids, to direct a viewer through their composition.

# ASSIGNMENT 1.2

Find and photocopy two examples for each of the five types of visual linking concepts presented. Label them appropriately and paste in your sketchbook.

## GRIDS

The word "design" implies that the various components of a visual image are organized into a cohesive unified composition. The third concept used to help unify a composition is the grid.

A grid is a network of horizontal (X) and vertical (Y) intersecting lines that divide the page and create a framework of areas. It is the most adaptable and universally applicable of all systems. Grids provide a sense of continuity, either between a series of elements in a single composition, or in multiple designs, as in a series of related paintings, prints, or in the layout of books, magazines, and websites. The purpose of the grid is to present the set of pictures or pages so they look unified as a whole, while varying them enough to make them interesting.

When the grid is equally shaped, as in a checkerboard pattern, we can readily see the repetition of shapes and the obvious continuation of lined-up edges. The downside to the checkerboard grid is that it tends to be a bit boring and predictable. Adding some variation, such as combining more than one section and repeating this procedure throughout the grid, can help ease some of this boredom. Stretching the grid horizontally or vertically is another technique that will add even more visual interest while still maintaining a sense of unity in the composition.

In art and design, grids are a way of analyzing works as well as organizing shapes and colors into some sort of unity. Grids can be used to divide any format into innumerable areas or modules. In creating the original grid, there are often numerous technical considerations that would determine the solution. But the basic idea is easily understood. The unifying power of a grid is so great that even the most disparate information gains cohesion when a grid is used. When dealing with grids, it is important to remember that, with a great variety of elements, a simple layout idea can give the needed unity and be very effective.

Grids can be used many different ways. Since their pattern need not be based on identical spaces but can depend upon any regulated distance of vertical, horizontal, or diagonal elements, many possibilities are open to designers using them. They can be used to expand an idea as well as to increase the size of an artwork.

One of the most exciting areas in design currently is web design. Web pages are often structured on a predetermined template that acts as a grid. Art whose application conforms to a specific procedure and adheres to a body of rules is sometimes referred to as systemic art. Grids alone are not enough to guarantee a successful composition, as can be seen in the range of quality in web page designs. To separate your web design from the masses, practice, learn, and apply the concepts covered in this textbook.

# ASSIGNMENT 1.3

Make a photocopy of a work of art or a magazine page. Tape a sheet of tracing paper over top of it and insert them into your sketchbook. On the sheet of tracing paper, deconstruct the image into a grid and depict how an artist used the alignment of the X- and Y-axes to unify a composition.

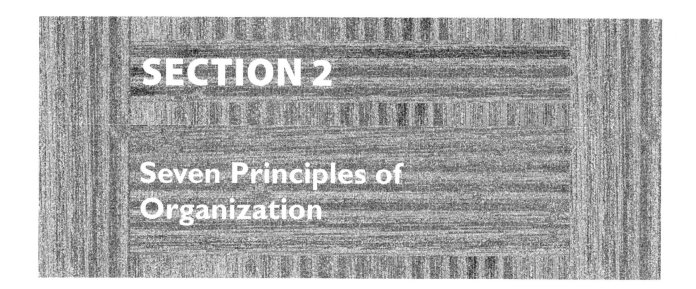

# SECTION 2

## Seven Principles of Organization

## SEVEN PRINCIPLES OF VISUAL ORGANIZATION

Before we break the rules, we must first appreciate what they are, why they exist, where they come from, and how they work.

The principles of arranging and organizing the elements into an aesthetically pleasing composition have been developed over the centuries, either intuitively or according to mathematical and quasi-scientific methods. This section is an introduction and guide to understanding the principles of organization.

The foundations of composition are harmony and variety. They are the antithesis of one another and together form the basis from which design is built. Developing an effective relationship between them is imperative to the success of a composition. Harmony pulls the compositional components together and makes them readable and coherent. Variety brings unpredictability to the compositional components and adds excitement and vitality to a design.

# HARMONY

© Stelian Ion, 2014. Used under license with Shutterstock, Inc.

Harmony may manifest as the dominance of one visual idea, a feeling of interconnected relationships, an obvious pattern, or a rhythmic movement. The principle of harmony involves the introduction of a repeated commonality, such as line, shape, texture, value, or color, to each of the compositional components. Harmony is a necessary ingredient in achieving overall unity within a design. Repetition and rhythm are two ways to introduce harmony into a composition.

## Repetition

Repetition is simply the reproduction of an art element (line, shape, texture, value, and color) and the characteristics of an art element (angles, directional patterns, or motifs) into the various parts of a design. The intent of repetition is to unify all of the compositional components by giving them similar characteristics. Even though any of the art elements can be repeated, the repetition of color is most commonly used to unify a design. The most successful harmonies are those created by repetition, in which all of the possible variables of art elements are the same. Repetition helps develop a sense of order and wholeness for the viewer and infuse the composition with a degree of harmony.

A composition with repeated elements, and or designs, that are usually varied and produce interconnections and obvious directional movement is called a pattern.

Pattern is usually seen as a noticeable formation or set of characteristics that is created when the basic configuration is repeated. A motif is closely related to pattern. A pattern is repetition of unit, cell, or original motif. A motif is a design unit that is repeated often enough in the total composition to make it a significant theme or dominant feature creating the pattern.

In the image above, harmony is developed through the repetition of the circular shape and the color blue.

# Rhythm

© Frank Rohde, 2014. Used under license with Shutterstock, Inc.

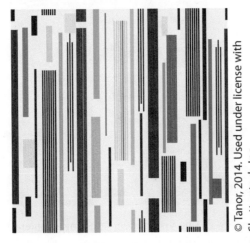

© Tanor, 2014. Used under license with Shutterstock, Inc.

Rhythm is the second way of establishing harmony in a composition. It is an elaboration of repetition and is based on the grouping of similar items. Rhythm is a continuance, a flow, or a sense of movement achieved through sustained repetition of the same element or two or more elements. In a more extensive arrangement, rhythm can be described as the cadence of a pattern.

Rhythm is created by the movement of the viewer's eyes across or around a composition, taking in the repetition of elements that have been placed with some kind of structured variation. When a viewer's eye moves quickly and easily from one compositional element to another, the visual pattern that structures the viewer's eye movement is called visual rhythm. Visual rhythm can be repeated lines, shapes, textures, values, or colors. How an artist manipulates the art elements in a composition determines how the viewer's eye moves across recurrent motifs. When art elements are used this way, they become visual connecting forces. Either real or implied, these visual connecting forces guide the viewer through a design, influence how long they pause, as well as determine where their eye goes next. Shapes and their arrangement are responsible for most of the rhythmic repetition in compositions.

Rhythm in art and design relies on the reiteration of elements or motifs that have been strategically positioned around the picture plane and selectively embellished to suit the artist's intended hierarchy. Repetitive divisions alone do not constitute a rhythm. It is necessary to set up a balance between a regular element and irregularities, between a major dominant element and the minor variants. Like rhythm in music, visual rhythms provide direction to the viewer. The rhythm can be smooth and lengthy without breaks (legato) or characterized by short and abrupt (staccato) breaks. Rhythmic patterning will elevate elements into a higher order of relatedness. However, repetition can quickly become predictable and monotonous. When this happens, a viewer becomes bored and visually dismisses the art.

Rhythm depends on contrast, which may be between horizontal, vertical, and diagonals lines, between geometric and biomorphic shapes, or between slow, smooth, and fast hectic transitions as the eye is directed around the picture. It is achieved in the same ways we create emphasis, but with the extra dimension of progression.

Higher order patterns can be created by varying any of the elements—position, size, shape, color, or texture—and in a variety of modes: regular or irregular, formal or informal, romantic or classical, free or constrained. Similarly, we see rhythm in the relative spacing of elements within a painting, sculpture, or building. Repetition alone is not enough to create a visually engaging piece. The real and implied lines or lost and found edges created by the shape and direction of elements, Gestalt groupings, and motifs linked by association, sometimes allow us to cruise along comfortably, but then we are forced to leap over precipitous gaps. The pace of our journey is controlled by the composition's rhythm.

Movement and rhythm go hand in hand. With the exception of kinetic sculpture and the time-based arts, we are attempting to create the illusion of movement on a two-dimensional surface or in the three-dimensional form of a sculpture.

Introducing rhythm to an artwork or design adds a touch of finesse and can turn an accomplished composition into an exceptional one. Alternation and progression are two types of rhythm used to breathe life into a design.

The concept of alternating rhythm is quite simple. Developed rhythmic visual patterns are constructed from two or more contrasting elements and arranged in a regularly repeating and interchanging manner. Alternating rhythm is a rhythm of two motifs that vary with one another to produce a regular, and soon anticipated, sequence. Here, a viewer's anticipation and expectations are not considered a fault in the design, but its strength to be exploited in helping to unify the composition. Alternating rhythm is often used in architectural designs because it appears familiar and develops a sense of safety and uniformity. Because alternating rhythm is so simple, it tends to be boring and must be selectively introduced into a design.

The second type of rhythm in design is progressive rhythm. Again, the rhythm involves repetition, but in this case, it is created through regular changes in a repeated element, such as a series of circles that progressively increase or decrease in size. This type of rhythm is reminiscent of growth patterns found in nature. Progressive rhythm is often achieved through sequential pattern variations of the size of a shape, through its color, value, or texture being the varying element. The gradual increase in size and weight creates a visual movement upward and outward. Progressive rhythm is commonplace in nature and extremely familiar to us. It too can sometimes become monotonous.

Repetition and rhythm can bring both excitement and harmony, depending on how they are used. Awareness of repetition, rhythm, and pattern cannot exist without similarity grouping. Similarity grouping is a function of visual intelligence that identifies relationships of parts and their place in the order of the whole.

In this section, we learned that harmony can unify a composition, but that too much harmony is detrimental to maintaining a viewer's interest. In the next section, we will explore the second foundation of the principles of organization: variety. Variety adds excitement, interest, and gradually breathes life into a design.

The two examples above illustrate two diverse rhythms. The image of red circles is very consistent and predictable, making it feel safe to the viewer. On the other hand, the image of vertical lines is unstable and may make the viewer feel uneasy.

# VARIETY

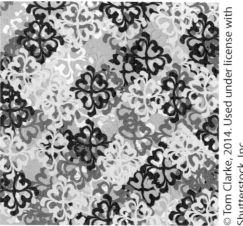

Variety is defined as the difference achieved by opposing, contrasting, changing, elaborating, or diversifying elements in a composition to add individualism and interest.

Variety is considered the opposite of harmony. They have a codependent relationship. One is stable but a bit boring, and the other is a bit scattered but fun. Together they coexist and complement each other on the picture plane.

In a composition, the introduction of variety enables the artist to present his individualistic point of view by challenging what he has established as the norm of harmony. Introducing variety is essential to capturing and maintaining a viewer's visual interest.

Harmony was explained as a cohesive force that keeps the art elements together. This is not the case with variety. It is responsible for visually separating or the pulling apart of the related art elements and challenging harmony. The relationship between harmony and variety does not need to be equitable. Either one may be greater in a composition. Anomaly, contrast, and elaboration are three ways in which variety can be introduced into a composition. The artist's intent or idea will determine the level in which variety will engage harmony.

An anomaly is a deviation from the normal or expected form, order, or arrangement. Incorporating one or more anomalies into an artwork provides a subtle but noticeable change in a design. The second way that variety or dissimilarity is introduced is elaboration. It is the subtle addition of minute details or embellishments to areas that lack visual interest. Elaboration intentionally introduces individual difference or opposition. The third way variety is introduced to a design is through contrast. Contrast is more aggressive than an anomaly. It involves repeating elements in such a way that they appear disjointed or unrelated. It is characterized by an abrupt change and if used excessively throughout a design it will create a sense of visual chaos in the viewer.

For an artist, one of the most difficult concepts to become comfortable with is that of applying harmony and variety simultaneously to the same components. A strong understanding of harmony's and variety's functions and their relationship to one another is crucial to developing a strong foundation to successfully utilize balance, movement, proportion, dominance, and economy in a composition.

In the image above, the variety of color and overlapping diamonds creates visual interest that keeps the viewer engaged with the harmonious repetition of the diamond shapes.

# ASSIGNMENT 2.1

Find and photocopy two artworks and explain in writing how the concepts harmony and variety function within the artwork. Identify and explain which type of harmony and/or variety is developed and how. For example, when describing harmony, are both rhythm and repetition present? If so, how? Insert both the photocopies and your essays into your sketchbook and properly label them.

# BALANCE

## BALANCE

All of our lives, we observe balance in the world around us. In art, a viewer perceives balance as visual judgments based on their innate sense of balance in their bodies and past experiences. A lack of balance disturbs us.

In art, balance involves an equal distribution of visual weight on the picture plane. In accessing pictorial balance, we always assume a center, vertical axis, and usually expect to see some kind of equal weight (visual weight) distribution on either side. Within the picture plane, an artist needs to be aware of two types of balance that occur. The vertical balance horizontally divides the picture plane into top and bottom sections of the dividing axis. In general, the higher the distribution of visual weight or interest, the more unstable and dynamic the image becomes. This section will mainly focus on the second type, horizontal balance, which is the balance left and right of the vertical dividing axis.

The concept of balance refers to the placement or distribution of the visual weight or the force among visual units. All parts of the picture plane contribute to its visual balance, regardless of their size, shape, or visual weight. This also includes the figure (or positive shapes) and the ground (or negative shapes). Balance in a composition shifts each time a visual element is added or subtracted. Even very minor changes can substantially shift a composition's balance. The goal of an artist is to adjust the visual weight of the elements so they appear to be in equilibrium.

It is impossible to develop a sense of compositional unity without balance. Balance is present the moment an artist makes her first mark on the page.

As a viewer's eye travels over the picture surface, it pauses momentarily at the significant points of interest determined by the artist. These points of interest develop movement or directional forces that counterbalance one another. While balancing a composition, an artist needs to be attentive to the placement of these points of interest and the tension they develop.

Visual weight can be defined in two ways. First, visual weight refers to the inclination of shapes to float or sink within the picture plane. Second and more importantly, visual weight can refer to the relative importance of a visual element within a composition.

The compositional forces that most influence visual weight are size, value, type of shape, texture, location, and orientation. The context in which a visual unit is placed strongly affects each of these forces.

When a shape is placed on a neutral white ground, darker values and vigorous textures generally increase its visual weight. Circles tend to stand out when placed in a rectangular format, while squares are less noticeable. A shape's visual weight is also affected by the placement within the picture plane. Shapes that appear to extend beyond the upper edge tend to rise, while shapes that appear to extend below the bottom appear to sink. Even the most abstract design is governed by gravity.

## Pictorial Balance

In assessing pictorial balance, we always assume a center vertical axis and usually expect to see some kind of equal weight (visual weight) distribution on either side. Each type of balance has its advantages. There are even some cases in which a degree of imbalance is necessary.

Some equal distribution of visual weight is a universal aim of composition. The artist has consciously balanced the vast majority of pictures we see. However, this does not mean there is no place in art for purposeful imbalance. An artist may, because of a particular theme or topic, express desire that a picture raise uneasy and disquieting responses in the viewer. In this instance, imbalance can be a useful tool.

We are almost always referring to horizontal balance, the left and right sides of the image, when referring to the pictorial balance. When an artist uses vertical balance, the farther up the main distribution of weight or visual interest occurs in the picture plane, the more unstable and dynamic the image becomes.

## Five Types of Balance

There are five types of balance and each one involves configuring the art elements differently by varying their position or placement, proportion, character, and direction. Of these factors, placement or position is the most important. The five types of balance are formal/symmetrical, approximate symmetrical, informal/asymmetrical, radial, and crystallographic.

### Formal/Symmetrical Balance

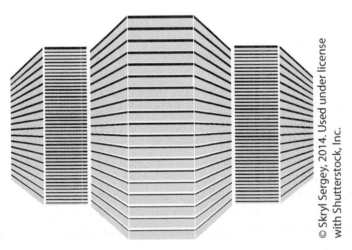

© Skryl Sergey, 2014. Used under license with Shutterstock, Inc.

Formal balance has equal or similar elements placed on opposite sides of the central axis. Its design layout tends to be very geometrically based and very mathematically divisible visually. It is the easiest type of balance to recognize and construct. Most public buildings are formally balanced because architects want them to be perceived as being permanent and dignified.

Symmetrical balance is a special type of formal balance and has true symmetry. It is also referred to as a mirror image. A symmetrical image can be divided by horizontal, vertical, or diagonal line and the image will appear equal on either side of the axis. Symmetrical balances create strong emphasis in the middle of the composition. Bilateral symmetry balances, developed along the horizontal axis, tend to be perceived as top heavy. To counter this, more visual weight can be emphasized in the lower portion of the picture plane. The background area between the figure and the picture frame are important and need to be considered in symmetrically balanced designs. The terms "formal" and "symmetrical" have become interchangeable in discussing design. Throughout the remainder of this textbook, formal balance will be referred to as symmetrical balance.

In symmetrical artworks, the main subject or object is placed in the very center of the picture plane and all of the other elements are equally distributed along its axis. This limited visual movement can appeal to our desire for equilibrium. When the axis is orientated vertically, symmetrical designs can convey a sense of calmness, dignity, and stability. Horizontal-axis-based images can be perceived as aggressive and intimidating. Sometimes, the subject matter makes symmetrical balance appropriate and more than a simple design solution.

Inverted symmetry and biaxial symmetry are two other types of symmetrical designs. Inverted symmetry has a symmetry with one half inverted. This type of design is used in playing cards. The other symmetrical design is called biaxial symmetry. It uses two axes of symmetry, vertical, and horizontal, which guarantee top and bottom balance, as well as left and right balance. Top and bottom can be the same on the left and right or they can be different. It is also possible to have more than two axes; snowflakes and kaleidoscopes, for example, have three axes of symmetry. When there is too much symmetry, however, we enter the realm of patterning.

Although symmetrical designs are unified, they do not always maintain the viewer's attention. To alleviate this problem, an artist can increase a viewer's interaction time by inserting secondary decorative details or changing his balance approach to one more suitable to his design needs.

# ASSIGNMENT 2.2

Find and photocopy two symmetrical compositions and insert them into your workbook. With words, dissect and explain how these compositions work visually and why the balance is congruent with the artist's intent.

## Approximate Symmetrical Balance

Approximate symmetry is basically symmetrical design with a bit of flexibility. It is characterized by the appearance of similar imagery being placed along side of the central axis, but the two sides are not perfectly identical—although the apparent visual weights of the components still are visually balanced.

Although these differences add variety and produce more visual interest, these images still appear fairly static. Approximate symmetry requires more sensitivity from the artist regarding the various weights for placement, proportion, character, and direction.

# ASSIGNMENT 2.3

Find and photocopy two approximate symmetrical compositions and insert them into your workbook. With words, dissect and explain how the composition works visually and why approximate symmetry was the appropriate balance choice.

# Informal/Asymmetrical Balance

Informal or asymmetrical balance involves creating a sense of visual equilibrium through the organization of dissimilar objects, while maintaining an overall harmony. This type of balance is dynamic and more exciting than formal balance (hence the alternate title of informal balance) but requires more imagination and design knowledge. Depending on the degree of asymmetry, the resulting design may range from quite stable to very dynamic or nearly chaotic.

Although informal compositions may appear unplanned, they require more thought than symmetrically dividing the picture plane. One way is to divide the picture plane into thirds. Important items are placed where these vertical and horizontal dividing lines intersect. Asymmetrical balance often uses the Golden Mean rule as a way to divide the picture plane into visually pleasing proportions. Even though it is an introductory concept to dividing a composition, the Golden Mean or sometimes referred to as Golden Section is a useful concept to know. It will be discussed further in depth in the chapter on Scale and Proportion.

In attempting to balance elements asymmetrically, an artist may use a combination of many attributes to distribute visual interest around the canvas so that the overall effect is one of equilibrium. In a successfully executed informal design, the viewer should not be aware of how balance was achieved. Dissimilar elements on a picture plane can be balanced by following some simple guidelines.

There are many ways to achieve asymmetrical balance. A small, visually interesting object can balance a much larger, less interesting object or an area of negative space. The size, shape, color, texture, value, and placement of the elements must be carefully and creatively adjusted before balance can be achieved. In an asymmetrical arrangement, the negative space is as important as the positive and must be equally considered in balancing the composition.

Asymmetrical balance becomes even more interesting when enclosed by a picture frame. The addition of the picture frame activates the negative space, which now becomes just as important as each positive shape. This enables more complex compositions to be created. For example:

1. A small shape placed near the bottom of the format balances a large shape placed along the top. Especially within a tall rectangle, shapes placed near the top tend to rise, while shapes placed near the bottom tend to sink.
2. When a small shape interacts with the bottom edge of the frame and a large shape moves away from the edge, the difference in their visual weight becomes even more pronounced. The larger shape will loose its visual weight and the smaller shape will gain visual weight.
3. A small visually complex shape placed toward the left or right picture frame will balance a larger less complex shape because it commands more of the viewer's attention.

# ASSIGNMENT 2.4

Find and photocopy two examples for each of the three picture frame asymmetrical compositions described above and insert them into your workbook. With words, explain how the asymmetrical compositional balance is developed visually in each example.

# Eight Ways to Achieve Asymmetrical Balance

1. Position

   Two items of unequal weight can be brought to equilibrium by moving the visually heavier inward toward the fulcrum. In design, this means that a smaller item placed out toward the edge of the picture plane can balance a large item placed closer to the center of the page. Balance by position often lends an unusual, unexpected quality to the composition. The effect not only appears casual and unplanned but also can make the composition seem, at first glance, to be imbalanced.

2. Solid

   A smaller solid shape will have more visual weight than a larger outlined shape.

3. Visual Complexity

   Complicated contours will attract more attention. A small, visually interesting object can balance a much larger, less interesting object or an area of negative space. A shape with jagged or undulating edges or one that is not easily recognizable will have more visual weight than a simple or common shape such as a circle or rectangle.

4. Texture

   A small shape of interesting texture can balance a larger area of less visual interest. Squinting your eyes helps identify the visual weights of texture surface. Any visual texture with a variegated dark and light pattern holds more interest for the eye than does a smooth, uninterrupted, consistent surface.

5. Color

   Our eye gravitates toward shapes with color. Some colors have a higher visibility than others—red and yellow, for example. The environment in which a color is placed has a tremendous effect on the color's visual weight. Colors' visual weights may be accentuated if they are placed beside, or surrounded by, their complementary color.

   If a painting looks perfectly balanced in color, but off-balance when it is reproduced in black and white, we know that color has played its part. In the most successful compositions, all the balancing strategies will work in concert. A painting in which the position, size, and direction of shapes suggest a dynamic, asymmetrical design can be "slowed down" by a careful distribution of colors.

6. Value

   Our eyes are naturally going to approach a light value against a predominantly dark background or a dark mass that is surrounded by lighter space. The higher the contrast the more we are attracted, the more the visual weight. As in similar cases of shape and texture, a small, intense area can balance a larger, more diffused area. Generally, a dark shape feels heavier than a light one of the same size, and a smaller dark shape can balance a larger light one. A relatively small area with high contrast on one side of the picture can balance a larger one of various grades closely related in value.

7. Grouping

   In the same way a small shape placed close to the outer edge may balance a centrally located larger shape on the picture plane, two or more small shapes can balance a larger one.

8. Connecting the Eyes

   With connecting the eyes, balance is created by the subtle eye direction of the people positioned in the composition. Although not usually the only technique of balance employed by an artist, eye direction is a commonly used device. Eye direction is carefully plotted, not only for balance but also for general compositional unity.

   Figures in paintings have eyes and are generally looking at something. The implied lines that join the eye to the object being looked at attract our attention—we are curious to know what the characters are looking at and implied lines and extended edges link objects and help unify a composition. Implied lines also have a "magnetic" effect on the weight and position of a figure or object. If someone is looking away from the center of the painting—out of the frame for example—we feel their shape drifting toward the edge of the picture. If someone is looking into the picture, their shape will be pulled toward the center of the image. It is as if we anticipate them moving toward the object of their gaze.

Similarly, the orientation and shapes of objects being viewed by the "eyes" can have their perceived position altered, thus upsetting or reinforcing the balance of the composition. If an object is depicted in the act of moving, its projected position is therefore as important as its actual, frozen position on the canvas.

## Summary

Isolating one technique of asymmetrical balance, as we have done, is a bit misleading because the vast majority of works employ several of the methods simultaneously. Principles often overlap and are frequently used together.

# ASSIGNMENT 2.5

Find, photocopy, and insert into your sketchbook two examples for each of the eight ways visual balance can be achieved in an asymmetrical design. Briefly write an explanation describing the balance of the composition technically and how and why it relates to the subject matter.

## Radial Balance

Radial balance is a form of symmetry in which elements radiate from a center point, either in straight lines toward the edge of a circle or spiraling outward like the seeds at the center of a sunflower. These lines and shapes are mirrored both vertically and horizontally, with the center of the composition acting as a focal point. Radial patterns can also be centrifugal (radiating from outside to inside) or concentric (like a target).

Radial balance is not entirely distinct from symmetrical or asymmetrical balance. It is merely a refinement of one or the other, depending on whether the focus occurs in the middle or off-center. The image below is an example of asymmetrical radial balance.

A popular variant on radial balance is the spiral. A spiral can increase energy in a circular format or add movement to a rectangular composition.

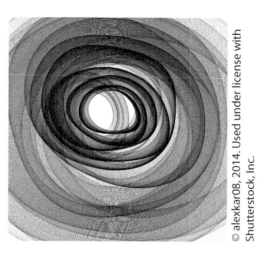

Radial balance has been used frequently in architecture and graphic arts. Such a design immediately focuses the viewer's attention and gives emphasis to the center as a place of functional significance. The advantage of such a design is the clear emphasis on the center and the unity that this form or design suggests.

# ASSIGNMENT 2.6

Find two examples of artworks that use a radial balanced design and write a brief paragraph explaining how and why it is appropriate for the subject matter.

# Crystallographic Balance or Allover Pattern

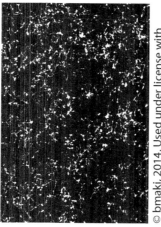

Crystallographic or allover pattern is characterized by compositions having the same degree of visual attraction distributed uniformly across the surface of the painting or print. The lack of emphasis causes our eyes to wander aimlessly all over the picture plane, intrigued by the apparent lack of emphasis. There is no beginning, no end, and no focal point—unless, indeed, the whole is the focal point.

This technique is, of course, a rather special refinement of symmetrical balance. The constant repetition of the same quality everywhere on the surface however creates an impression truly different from our usual concept of symmetrical balance. The usual concept of balancing elements does not apply when every element is equally stressed in visual importance. Fabric patterns and wall paper purposefully lack any focal point and are usually distinguished by a constant repetition of the same motif.

# ASSIGNMENT 2.7

Find two examples of artworks that use either crystallographic or allover pattern balanced designs and write a brief paragraph explaining how and why this balance is appropriate for the subject matter.

# FOCAL POINT/EMPHASIS/DOMINANCE

## FOCAL POINT/EMPHASIS/DOMINANCE

The focal point is anywhere your eye comes to rest when viewing a compositional design.

Emphasis is when special attention or embellishment is given to an element, characteristic, or object in a work of art so that it stands out visually.

Dominance is when certain elements assume more importance than others within the same composition. Dominance's main compositional contribution is to create an entry point to lead the viewer to other parts of the composition. Once in the design, so to speak, emphasis or focal points then lead the viewer to the other parts of the composition. Both emphasis and focal points attract attention and increase the composition's visual and conceptual impact.

When you create dominance in your artwork, you are creating elements that command attention and prevail over the other elements. In a successful composition, the designer will create subordinate (secondary) and supportive (tertiary) dominance. As these names suggests, they are visual clues given to the viewer for them to follow as they continue to explore the composition. Dominance relies on contrast to attract the viewer's attention.

© IgorGolovniov, 2014. Used under license with Shutterstock, Inc.

It is the artist's responsibility to ensure that there is a consistency between her intent and the composition. The art elements' individual roles may vary in terms of importance, but all must work in unison. The unified narrative that she intends is conveyed by controlling the focal points, emphasis, and dominance of the art elements. There are three levels of dominance that can be identified in a composition—dominant, subordinate, and supportive—and all are used to help clarify the artist's intent visually.

1. Dominant. The dominant element is the one (or ones) given the most visual weight. It is the primary emphasis of the composition and often exists in the foreground of the picture plane. It reveals what is

51

most important and indicates where a viewer should first look. In the example above, the large picture of Stalin behind the standing military figures is clearly the dominant element in this image.

2. Sub-dominant. This is the middle level and is secondary in importance. A viewer searches out these focal points after the dominant ones have been acknowledged. In the image above, the military figures standing in the center of the image would be considered sub-dominant elements.

3. Subordinate. These are elements with a tertiary emphasis and are given the least visual weight. Subordinate elements recede into the background of a design. This would include all of the remaining elements in the image above.

Art elements compete with each other for attention in compositions that lack dominance. This lack of defined elements confuses viewers because they do not know how to move through a composition. When this happens, viewers usually lose interest. As a rule, the art elements with the most visual weight will be the most dominant. The following guidelines explain how to create dominance in your design.

You can add more visual weight to individual art elements through:

1. Size. The larger a shape's size, the more dominance it possesses.
2. Color. Some colors command more visual attention than others. Red is perceived as having the most visual power and yellow the least.
3. Density. The more densely packed elements are into a given space, the more visual weight in that area.
4. Value. A darker element has more weight than a lighter object.
5. Foreground. The objects in the foreground have more visual weight or dominance than those in the background.

Visual weight is a combination of all of the above. The biggest element on the page might be of the lightest color and still recede into the background.

# ASSIGNMENT 2.8

In your sketchbook, find and insert two examples of artwork that depict varying degrees of emphasis. On an overlay piece of tracing paper, use highlighter pens to define the three levels of emphasis that are depicted.

Now you should have a better understanding of how the characteristics of individual art elements can be manipulated to create dominance. The next section will explain how dominance can be achieved through the art elements' relationship to the picture plane.

## 1. Emphasis by Isolation

The odd one out always demands our attention, and one of the easiest ways to create emphasis is to isolate an element from all the others, either by separating it physically or by making it symbolically different. These symbolic themes can be supported by careful placement, by scale, and by the choice of color. This is contrast of course, but it is contrast of placement, not form. Isolating an element involves placing it apart from the other elements and thereby creating a focal point.

## 2. Emphasis by Placement

An artist designs a composition to control a viewer's attention. Unless otherwise controlled, the viewer's eyes will naturally come to rest in the center of the picture plane. The center of the page is where the most important information is normally placed. Isolating and placing an element in the middle area would catch the viewer's attention. This practice is usually criticized and perceived as being naïve because it is such an obvious solution.

The other compositional elements function in a supporting role and help create emphasis. If their placement points in a specific direction, then that area will be emphasized and the viewer's attention will be directed there. This concept is the basis of a radial design. The viewer's attention is directed inward to the center area repeatedly. It is important that all the elements support the area designated as the main focal point to avoid confusion of the emphasis. The priority of any design is visual unity and should not be sacrificed just to develop a focal point.

## 3. Emphasis by One Element

A specific theme may at times call for a dominant, even visually overwhelming, focal point. The use of a strong individual emphasis on one element is not unusual. This approach is often used in graphic design, billboards, and magazine covers.

## 4. Emphasis by Contrast

As a rule, a focal point results when one element differs from the others. Whatever interrupts an overall feeling or pattern automatically attracts the eye by this difference. Contrast is created when two or more forces operate in opposition. The list of possible ways to contrast two design elements could fill several books. An 80/20 ratio between contrasting forces tends to create an effective and pleasing composition. The larger portion will establish the norm while the smaller portion becomes the diversion.

The objective of contrast is to produce maximum visibility of the dominant feature. The more contrast there is, the more noticeable an item is. Contrast can be achieved through varying direction, color, texture, character, size, value, and so on.

Whatever interrupts an overall feeling or pattern will automatically attract the eye by this very difference. The more complicated the pattern, the more necessary or helpful a focal point, created by contrast, may become in organizing the design. These contrasting elements provide the viewer with a place to rest.

## 5. Emphasis through Scale and Proportion

Scale and proportion are used to create emphasis, expression, and to suggest spatial positions. Having elements of differing sizes develops visual interest in a composition, and scale has a huge impact on emphasis. Bigger is better, in most cases. Certainly, shapes and forms that are larger than other elements have a greater visual presence. Most often, the size and scale of an artwork are dictated by its intended location and use. Scale can be unexpected or exaggerated to draw our attention. For example, when small objects are magnified or large ones are reduced they command more of the viewer's attention.

## 6. No Focal Point

If you cannot find an obvious center of attention in a painting or drawing, the picture as a whole becomes the focal point. Two kinds of images fall into this category: big, busy scenes with so much going on that no particular focal point dominates and nonobjective paintings or sculptures where the elements that make up the composition are so subservient to the whole that they melt into insignificance.

When developing a composition in which the focus is on the whole over the parts, establishing a definite focal point is not a necessity to a successful design, because it has no starting or visual ending. For example, shapes and textures can be loosely organized into a grid-like form of rows and columns with the intent of creating an ambiguous and puzzling visual environment. Here, the repetition and suggested continuation beyond the edge of the composition emphasize the whole over the parts. However, emphasis of the whole over any one part is not limited to simple repeated geometric patterns.

## Design Concerns About Emphasis

The creation of a harmonious pattern with related elements is more important than the injection of a focal point, if this point jeopardizes the design's unity.

While you want to create dominance in your design to serve as a focal point, you still want the rest of your design to be experienced and contribute to the overall success of the composition. You want your design to be balanced overall. An element might be dominant simply because many of the other elements lead the viewer's eye to that area. When working to obtain dominance, many artists experience two problematic situations. First, they must ensure that each element has the proper degree of importance. Second, there must be a balance between the dominant and subordinate elements while achieving a unified work of art.

# ASSIGNMENT 2.9

Find two compositions for each of the six aforementioned concepts and describe in writing how the visual hierarchy of the subject matter was developed and why the specific ways of creating dominance used by the artist was appropriate.

# PROPORTION/SCALE

## PROPORTION/SCALE

© bondgrunge, 2014. Used under license with Shutterstock, Inc.

Scale and proportion are related terms: both basically refer to size and strongly affect compositional balance and emotional impact. Scale refers to the overall size as compared to the human form and proportion refers to the relationship of the individual elements to one another with in the composition or sculpture.

Scale is essentially another word for size. "Large scale" is a way of saying big, and "small scale" means little. Either is relatively meaningless unless we have some standard of reference. Most of the time, this standard of reference is our own human body.

Artistically, scale can be considered several ways. What is the artwork's size in relation to other art, in relation to its surroundings, or in relation to human size? Unusual or unexpected scale is arresting and attention getting. Sheer size does impress us.

Proportion refers to the ratio of the elements as measured against the whole, the other elements, or against a mental norm or standard. Proportion is all about ratio. Again we could use the example of the human figure, where we would be concerned with the ratio of the sculpture's head to its overall height.

In past centuries, visual scale was often related to thematic importance. In early works of art, the size of the central figure relative to any others was a sign of its importance. Religious figures, such as saints, or kings or emperors were painted at a larger scale than the less important figures around them. This is called heretic scaling. Today, we are more likely to accept relative size as a depth cue: if a figure is bigger than the others, it must be closer to the viewer.

## Power of Unusual Scale

© Dragon Images, 2014. Used under license with Shutterstock, Inc.

The choice of scale and proportion is a major factor in achieving an artist's intention. First, both should be congruent to the theme presented in the artwork. For example, unusual scale in a work of art should have a thematic or functional justification. Bigness for the sake of bigness simply to gain attention is usually a mistake. If something is comparatively larger in proportion to the rest of the compositional components, it will have more importance. Second, both should be considered in relationship to the rest of the compositional elements and are governed by the principles of design.

If large or small size artworks develop naturally from the function, theme, or purpose of a work, an unusual scale is justified. For example, a small scale is appropriate to private reflection. Objects that are bigger than us diminish our perceived importance.

© Mayer George, 2014. Used under license with Shutterstock, Inc.

Scale within a work of art provides meaning, context, and often a clue as to how it was made. These visual clues affect how we interpret the image's or object's meaning. Cropping an image with the picture plane adds intimacy and spontaneity to a work of art. Scale is relative to the overall area of the format; a big element in one painting might be considered small in a larger work.

Some artists, however, use scale changes intentionally to intrigue or mystify us, rather than to clarify the focal point. An artist may purposely use scale to attract our attention in different ways. Big may startle us and small may provoke our curiosity.

# ASSIGNMENT 2.10

Find and photocopy two examples of artworks that use scale to visually communicate the artist's idea. In writing, briefly describe how and why scale was used for each example.

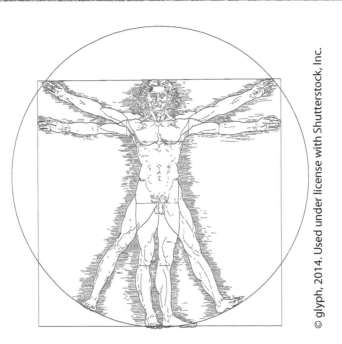

## Geometry and Notion of the Ideal

To speak of ideal proportions in the human body is difficult, because societies change their minds periodically about what constitutes human beauty. Most often, body proportions in works of art are purposely distorted for the sake of expression, to present an emotional image.

Proportion is a matter of personal judgment. While most artists today would reject any such rule, a form of the Golden Mean in composing their paintings has influenced certain classical artists of the past. The Golden Mean is a mathematical formula devised by the Greeks that expressed the view that mathematics was the controlling force of the universe. The Golden Mean, sometimes called the "Golden Section," represents the ideal standard for proportion and balance in life. It established for the Greeks the most harmonious ratios. As applied to works of art, it stated that a small part relates to a larger part as the larger part relates to the whole. For example, in geometric terms, a line AB divided by a line C will achieve the Golden Mean if AC to CB equals the proportion CB to AB. This ratio has a numerical value of 1.618. Any composition component added to or subtracted from the original unit will be this much smaller or larger than the original unit in a ratio of 1 to 1.618 (see example below).

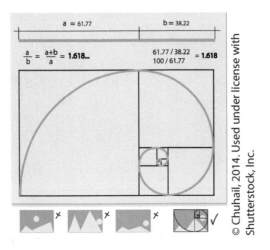

The Golden Mean is a proportion with seemingly magical properties and according to some, an in-built universal beauty. Although certainly a subjective judgment, the Golden Mean has influenced art and design throughout the centuries.

# ASSIGNMENT 2.11

Find and photocopy two artworks that use proportion as a means to develop content visually. In writing, briefly describe how and why proportion was used for each example.

# ASSIGNMENT 2.12

Find and photocopy two artworks that exemplify the Golden Mean division of space. Insert them into your sketchbook.

# MOVEMENT

In this textbook, movement is not the depiction or illustration of something moving within an artwork. Movement is considered the arrangement of the art elements to develop a path for the viewer's eye to follow while experiencing an artwork. These art elements are arranged according to the principles of organization to convey a sense of motion. An artist can repeat an element, vary the scale or proportion, or create differing values to develop the effect of movement in a visual artwork. For example, repeating an art element in different places within the composition often suggests the passing of time or movement.

© adamk78, 2014. Used under license with Shutterstock, Inc.

Visual movement drives the viewer's eye to focal points as well as ensures that all of the areas of composition are explored. Often the artist's goal is to create a visual loop to direct the viewer back into the composition repeatedly. Visual loops keep the viewer engaged in the artwork by not allowing his eyes to leave the picture plane.

# ASSIGNMENT 2.13

Find and photocopy two examples of designs that incorporate movement and explain in writing how movement is developed and why movement is an important conceptual component of the design.

# ECONOMY

## ECONOMY

Antoine de Saint-Exupery summarizes economy best, when he states: "Perfection is achieved, not when there is nothing more to add, but when there is nothing left to take away."

© Pablo Inones, 2014. Used under license with Shutterstock, Inc.

The principle of economy is based on the idea that you use only as much as you need in order to communicate the message visually. It applies to the overall artwork not just to a specific component. The easiest way to interpret economy is in terms of what can be removed. This does not mean that the design is minimalistic, but rather that it only contains the essential. If you can remove an element within a design and that design still works, then you have practiced economy in design. Economy is achieved when every art element is visually important and contributes to the overall success of the composition. An artist is forced to evaluate every element and analyze whether or not it is vital to the message. Do not offer more than is needed, but be sure to include all that is needed to create an intelligent and economical design.

Economy is used to achieve harmony, create focus and direction, and unify a design. To achieve economy the artist must have a clear understanding of what she is trying to convey. These clear and concise intentions help us evaluate and make appropriate compositional decisions. Knowing what to leave out is as important as knowing what to include. Using visual economy, we can distill a design down to its true essence.

# ASSIGNMENT 2.14

Find and photocopy two examples of artwork depicting the concept of economy. Insert them into your sketchbook. In writing, explain how each design element contributes to the overall success of the composition. Also, explain why the concept of economy is appropriate to the subject matter of the artwork. Identify and explain the contextual integration of the artist's idea and his choice of materials for the design.

# SECTION 3

## The Art Elements

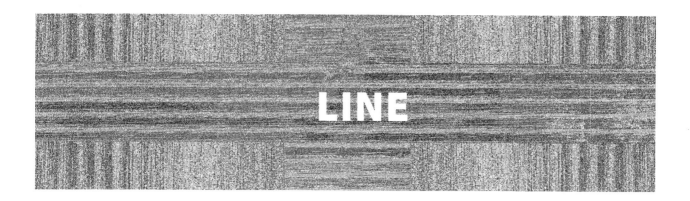

# LINE

Line, shape, texture, value, and color are the basic building blocks from which two-dimensional designs are made. These visual elements can exist independently as well as in combination. A point is the essence of design. It reflects the existence of a physical relationship between materials, the presence of thought, the expression of emotion, and the result of action.

## Point

Every design starts with a single point. You can physically change the perceived visual value of a piece of paper with just one dot, because of a process called optical mixing. This is a process in which your brain optically mixes elements it sees. Optical mixing will be further explained in the chapter on color.

A single point can be made with many tools, with different media, or with color—all of which will change its character as well as expand its potential to express an idea. When more than one point or a group of points are combined, they develop value and can be used to suggest form. This process is known as stippling.

## Line

Mathematically, a line is defined as a point (which is made by a tool, instrument, or medium) that has no dimensions, and which is set into motion and made visible because it contrasts in value with its surroundings. All of this is true in art and design, except that in art, a line is described as having width as well as length.

A line in its simplest form is a series of dots. Points aligned in the general direction of a line constitute a dotted line. It is possible to make a picture by carefully arranging many points.

Line is one of the simplest and most versatile elements of design. Line maybe defined as: a point in motion; a series of adjacent points; a connection between points; or an implied connection between points.

Of all the elements in art, line is the most familiar to us. Simply by drawing a line, we can activate a space, define a shape, or create a bridge between visual elements. Despite their apparent simplicity, lines can add structure, movement, and cohesion to all forms of compositions.

As an element in its own right, line can be used throughout a composition. It can be an actual, an implied, or a psychic line. It can express an artist's idea, become a shape, and be used to define space.

One of the strongest features of line is its power of suggestion. It is able to convey all sorts of moods and feelings. As artists and designers, we anthropomorphize the elements of art. Often we describe lines as being, for example, nervous, angry, happy, free, quiet, excited, calm, graceful, and with having so many more human qualities. The remainder of this chapter will: introduce the various types of lines and qualities of lines, explore the amazing power of suggestion inherent in this basic element, and describe it as a structural framework.

## Types of Lines in Composition

The difficulty of working with the art element "line" is in knowing what it is, how far it can be pushed, and when it stops being a line and becomes something else. When developing a composition, the three important types of lines that play a role in compositions are actual, implied, and psychic.

Actual lines are just real lines that are physically made using a medium. They may vary greatly in weight, character, complexity, or other qualities. An actual line may also be called an explicit line and will be elaborated on in more detail later in this section.

Sometimes, we see lines that do not exist and are only a series of points that the eye tends to automatically connect. Implied lines simply suggest connections and the viewer must become actively involved in compositions that are constructed using this type of line. In order to see them, you have to abandon the idea that the only lines that exist are those physically made by the artist. Fortunately, we have an innate propensity to seek visual unity and given enough clues, we will connect separate visual parts by filling in the missing pieces. This inclination to connect fragmentary information is called closure.

A psychic line is arguably a line, for it has no existence at all, not even intermittent points, and yet we feel a mental connection between two elements. It only exists in our imagination. This usually occurs when something points or we follow the subject's gaze in a composition. Artists and designers use psychic lines to guide viewers around a picture and direct their viewing experience.

# ASSIGNMENT 3.1

Find and photocopy two examples of artworks in which psychic lines are used within the composition to direct the viewer's gaze. Next explain in writing why the artist used a psychic line within the composition. Insert the images and your written explanations into your sketchbook.

## Physical Characteristics of Line and its Use in Art

Lines usually reflect the implement that made them and can be created from a plethora of media. Each tool or medium has the potential to create a variety of different meanings. As mentioned earlier, line is the most fundamental and versatile of all design elements. It is the first kind of mark children make, largely by virtue of the drawing implements they are presented with and because of what might be perceived as a natural movement of the hand.

Mathematically, line has only one dimension, length. In art and design, we know line can have varying widths as well. A line can be described in terms of its measure, direction, location, and character.

### Measure of Line

In this textbook, when we discuss the measure of a line, we are referring to the various lengths and widths in which a line can exist. If a line is long, it provides a sense of continuity. A short, choppy, broken line can suggest an agitated emotion; a thick line might reference laziness, abundance, or presence; a line that ebbs and flows might suggest a change or wavering.

# ASSIGNMENT 3.2

Find and photocopy two examples of artworks that depict the measure of line. Explain how and why you feel the measure of line is appropriately being used to develop content.

## Type of Line

Type refers to the "style" of the line. It is a physical description of the shared features of the line, the "sort of," or the "essence" of the line. There are many different types of lines. If a line continues in only one direction, it is straight. A straight line that is long and consistent can be thought of as rigid and/or inflexible. If a continuous change of direction occurs gradually, it is considered curved. A curved line can form an arc, become wavy, or turn into itself and form a spiral. A curvy line is generally seen as visually entertaining and depending on the rhythm, stimulating or relaxing, graceful or unstable. When a line changes directions in a measurable, sudden, and abrupt manner, it is considered angular; if as a line proceeds, it switches directions and makes sharply alternating patterns, it is considered a zigzag. Since our eyes adapt to its ever-changing directions, the rhythm in which an angular line changes directions will determine if it produces excitement or confusion in the viewer.

# ASSIGNMENT 3.3

Find and photocopy two examples of artworks that depict the "type" of line. Explain how and why you feel the type of line is appropriately being used to develop content.

75

## Line Direction

Line direction is an important characteristic that also needs to be considered on two different levels: as an element and as a pictorial arrangement.

The design element "line" as mentioned above can have length and direction. The line's direction of development can send different messages to the brain of the viewer. Horizontal lines can be used to symbolize quiet, repose, serenity, and perfect stability. This may be because we associate the state of being horizontal with being at rest or asleep. Vertical lines, like standing figures, denote potential for action or upward movement. They suggest happiness, hope, poise, and aspiration.

Diagonal lines are the most dynamic of all lines and are thought to generally suggest agitation and motion. Depending on the direction of their movement, they can be perceived as positive or negative in mood. Diagonals that start in the lower left corner and proceed across the page toward the upper right corner of the picture plane are thought to be positive in nature and produce uplifting and positive thoughts. Whereas diagonal lines originating in the upper left corner and moving across the composition in a downward motion conjure up thoughts of defeat and decline.

Since most picture frames are four-sided rectangles, some consider the first line an artist makes to actually be the fifth contributing line of a composition. Therefore any horizontal or vertical line within the composition is parallel to, and repetitious of, an edge of the format. Horizontal and vertical lines within a design are called stabilizers. These are elements that reduce any feeling of movement. With this in mind, it is easier to understand why there is a congruent relationship of stability between the horizontal and vertical lines of a composition and a tense and dynamic relationship between diagonals and the picture plane.

The direction of line is very important because in large measures, it controls the movements of our eyes while we view a picture. Our eye movements can facilitate the continuity of relationships among the various properties of the element and unify the composition. It also plays a major role in developing the emotional quality and message of the artwork.

# ASSIGNMENT 3.4

Find and photocopy two examples of artworks that depict the "direction" of line. Explain how and why you feel the direction of line is appropriately being used to develop content.

## Location

The location of a line can either enhance or diminish the measure, type, or direction of a line within the picture plane. The physical properties of line, in conjunction with its location on the pictorial page, will determine how a viewer perceives it psychologically.

A line located in the lower right hand corner of the picture plane might be perceived as emotionally heavy, burdensome, lifeless, somber, exhausted and reaching the end of a journey. That same line located in the upper left hand corner of the picture plane might be perceived as light hearted, young, inspirational, happy, and having just begun its journey.

Line serves two functions within the composition: first, it contributes to the overall expressive quality, and second, it contributes to the composition's sense of unity. All of line's attributes—measure, type, direction, and location—should work in unison. Seldom do all of the physical properties and expressive qualities of lines act in unison. For example, if an artist intends to convey an inspirational and dynamic energy then she might use a diagonal line located toward the upper portion of the picture plane. By doing so, the diagonal line can be perceived as positive, and the expressive quality and the physical location are in unison. Yet if the same diagonal line were located in the lower portion of the composition, then it might be perceived to be plunging and there would be a discrepancy between the expressive qualities and the physical location; hence, these two attributes of line would not be in unison.

# ASSIGNMENT 3.5

Find and photocopy two examples of artworks that depict the "location" of line. Explain how and why you feel the direction of line is appropriately being used to develop content.

## Character

The final physical property of line to be discussed is character. Different tools make distinctively different marks, each with its own unique characteristics and inherent qualities. The personality or emotional quality of these lines is greatly dependent on the nature of the medium and tools chosen to make the line. It is the artist's experience, intention, and skill that determine the appropriateness and effectiveness of a line's character to convey her original intent. A unified work of art is one in which the artist chose the appropriate medium, tool, and application to physically make the lines that express a congruent relationship to her original idea or intent.

# ASSIGNMENT 3.6

Find and photocopy two examples of artworks that depict the "character" of line. Explain how and why you feel the character of line is appropriately being used to develop content.

## The Expressive Quality of Line

Lines are often described in general terms of emotional states of the human condition. An artist understands this and uses it as a means to convey his intent to a viewer.

The physical properties of line from which an artist has to choose are infinite, but a match between the line quality and the expressive intent is essential. The linear technique an artist chooses produces the emotional and expressive qualities in the final pattern. Solid and bold, quiet and flowing, delicate and dainty, jagged and nervous, or any countless other possibilities will influence the line's effect on the viewer.

By themselves, lines have little emotional character, just the physical properties as discussed in the last section. Lines are a basic means of communication, but an artist uses lines in a more broadly communicative manner. Arranging them into a planned composition organizes the viewers' thoughts and feelings, and brings the artist's message to the forefront. Although lines may be admired separately, their real beauty lies in the relationship they establish in the form. This form can be representational or nonrepresentational.

## Relationship of Line to the Other Art Elements

Line is amazing. When you think of the foundations of art or the essence of design, everything can be deconstructed down to line. Physically, line is very closely related to all of the other elements. It can possess texture, value, and color, as well as create shapes.

### Line and Shape

Line is important to the artist because it can describe shape, and by shape, we recognize objects. It is capable of creating flat shapes, as well as suggesting forms. To make a shape, line is used to define an enclosed boundary. To suggest forms or masses, often outlines or contour lines are used. Similar to creating a shape, both form and mass use a line that follows the outermost limits of an object. A line is described as an explicit line when forms are clearly delineated by it. Cross-contour lines change width and direction to develop a shape into a form. Cross-contour lines reflect how a viewer's eye travels across an object. They add interior detail to an outline and help define the volume of the object.

### Line and Value

A line creates value as soon as the first mark is made on a page. An artist can create value with line by manipulating the width of the actual line. A thicker line will produce a darker value than a thin line. Groups of lines such as hatching or cross-hatching create areas differing in value from the background. As marks eliminate the white background of a page, a darker value is created due to optical mixing, a concept further explored in the chapter on color. Similar in concept, controlling the space between lines also affects value. Widely spaced lines appear lighter and closely spaced lines create a darker value—once again due to optical mixing. Beyond manipulating the line physically, an artist can affect the value of a line by changing the media, varying the ratio of the medium's mixture, or simply modifying the pressure applied to a tool.

# ASSIGNMENT 3.7

In your sketchbook, make 10 equally separated 1" x 1.5" rectangles aligned in a straight row. Within each of the 10 rectangles, create a value by only varying the space and thickness of the lines. Starting on the left, create your lightest value. As you proceed to the right, each successive rectangle should represent the next darkest value. Try to represent as full a value scale as possible.

## Line and Texture

Lines are often used to develop texture in an artwork. A visual representation of texture can be as simple and quick as creating a texture lift from the surface of an object—or as complex and time consuming as a photorealistic drawing. Often a texture is simply inherent in the medium chosen and the amount of it applied. The tools used to apply the medium, as well as the training, experience, and skill level at which a medium is handled, will also determine the results.

## Line and Color

Combining line and color together creates tremendous possibilities. Basically, you have all of the art elements' visual potentials and expressive possibilities combined. A line encircled is a shape and grouping lines together can create both value and texture. The only element of art that is missing is color to make the elements complete. Color has come to be identified with different emotional states and is a powerful composition force.

## Spatial Characteristics of Line

Just the mere placement of line on a page activates the picture plane. Items located above the centerline tend to be further back in space than those at the bottom. The physical size of the line can denote the space it occupies. Large lines tend to come forward while small lines tend to recede. Similarly, the largest part of a line will come forward and the smallest part of a line will recede. Diagonal lines disappear into space as they converge at the vanishing points. As explained in the previous section on line and value, groups of lines are capable of creating darker values that recede in space. Finally, lines can be made with color. Cool colors generally recede and warm colors advance. Line is complex and every component affects the line's location in space.

## Linear Division of the Composition

The first drawn line in a composition is considered by many to actually be the fifth line because of the rectangular composition format.

Multiple lines and line networks can add detail to a design and create a convincing illusion of space. If you were to repeatedly fold a rectangular piece of paper in half, then unfolded it, you would notice that the creases accurately divide the rectangle into intersecting quadrants and diagonal lines. Each of these lines represents a possible foundational structure through which the suggestion of a line created by the edges of objects or actual lines can be located to develop pathways to move a viewer though a composition. These horizontal and diagonal organizational lines provide the framework for artists to unify, elaborate, and simplify compositions.

## Line as Representation

The strongest visual feature of line is its power to communicate. It can signify and convey both abstract and realistic ideas and emotions. With a comparatively few strokes, an artist can describe the edges or contours of shapes, develop their form, and create and define the illusion of space.

Lines can be used to depict facts in a utilitarian manner or express action in a gestural sense. A technical drawing of a building would be an example of line being used in a utilitarian manner, whereas in a life drawing class, gestural lines are used to represent the energy of a pose.

# ASSIGNMENT 3.8

In your sketchbook, using only a line or lines, create nonrepresentational designs to suggest the following emotions: anger, happiness, sadness, contentment, rage, inferiority, embarrassment, tiredness, pensiveness, anxiety, hope, fear, submission, contemplation, and confusion.

## Line as Drawing

A composition can be called a drawing, regardless of the medium, when the main art element used is line. A drawing is more than two-dimensional lines or marks on a page; the lines or marks are a visual record of movement over time. There are two general types of line drawings: contour and gesture.

A contour line drawing is one in which a composition is represented only by a line. It is the most common use of line in art. Contour lines define both the inner and outer edges of a form. A contour line may ebb and flow as it defines the edges of objects represented. The weight of the line tells us about the subject and helps produce the illusion of three-dimensionality.

The other most common type of drawing is called a gesture drawing. In a gesture drawing, the outline all but disappears, leaving marks that show the freshness and dynamics of a scene or pose and the action of drawing, rather than a planned and accurate arrangement of shapes. Gesture drawings are not drawings of objects so much as drawings of movement, weight, and posture. Their intent is to capture the momentary changing aspects of the subject rather than recording nuances of form. In a gesture drawing, representing the action or dynamics of a subject is more important than accurately describing the object. Lines in a gesture drawing move freely within forms and tend to be created with more spontaneity than those in a contour line drawing. They are loosely constructed, quickly drawn attempts to capture the past, present, and future motion of a subject.

# ASSIGNMENT 3.9

Find and photocopy examples of artworks that use contour and gesture lines as a means of developing the subject matter. In writing, describe why this specific type of line was used to execute the drawing.

In addition to contour and gesture lines, groupings known as hatching, cross-hatching, and cross-contour maybe used to create drawings. Hatching uses groups of straight parallel lines to produce a range of grays. A larger range of value can be achieved through a process known as cross-hatching. Cross-hatching is more complex than hatching and uses a combination of crisscrossing lines to develop value and suggest three-dimensionality. Cross-contour lines can create an even more powerful illusion of three-dimensionality. Often created using curving parallel lines, cross-contours "map" surface variations across shapes or objects. Hatching, cross-hatching, and cross-contours are often combined to create a more visually complex drawing.

Whatever the intent—expression of human emotions, depiction of action, or communication of factual information—a line is an important element that artists structure within a picture plane. The best way to learn control of what line can do is to experiment with it.

# ASSIGNMENT 3.10

Find and photocopy two artworks that have a pronounced emotional content. Next, place an overlay of tracing paper on top of them and using only line or lines, convey the emotional content of the artwork. Use the subject matter to inspire your choice of line type, character, direction, location, and measure.

# SHAPE

Shape in its simplest form is any visually perceived area identifiably different from its background or other elements in the composition. It can be defined by an actual outline or by a difference in texture, color, or value. If a shape exists with a blurry and undefined border, it is said to have an implied boundary. It is called an amorphous shape when the shape's edges are barely discernable at all.

A shape can be perceived visually, but not actually exist physically, because of Gestalt theory. This principle first put forward by the German Gestalt psychologists about human visual perception states that our minds tend to "see" organized wholes, or forms, as a totality, before they perceive the individual parts. The human brain is good at inferring shapes from inadequate information and tends to insist on creating shapes from approximately related elements.

The terms shape and form are often used interchangeably. To avoid confusion, we will define them as two separate ideas. A shape is two-dimensional, inferring it only possesses width and height. Form is the physical bulk of a solid body of material that contains mass. It exists three-dimensionally and has width, height, and depth. Form can also be described as having mass and volume.

On the picture plane, mass is defined as a shape that appears to be developed three-dimensionally from the space surrounding it or has the illusion of a solid body of material. The illusion of mass is achieved by shading and lighting, or by overlapping and merging shapes. In sculpture and architecture, mass is the actual or apparent material substance and density of a form.

Mass can be thought of as positive space and volume as negative space contained within or surrounding the mass. Mass is the actual object while volume is considered the measurable area of defined or occupied space. Three-dimensionally, volume is the space occupied by the form or by the immediate surrounding space. For example, an empty vase has volume within its mass and volume surrounding it.

## Fibonacci Series

Throughout history, cultures have tried to understand the ways of the universe. Many of these attempts were mathematical in nature. The Golden Mean as explained earlier is a mathematical formula that describes ideal proportions. The Fibonacci Series is also mathematical system used to scientifically understand and explain forms found in nature.

In 1202, Leonardo Pisano, known by his nickname Fibonacci, introduced the decimal system and the use of Arabic numerals into Western Europe. Historically, Islamic culture has been reluctant to use representational art because it is perceived as an attempt to imitate God's work. Instead, geometric shapes are extensively used to create amazing patterns of beauty.

The Fibonacci series looks very simple, but is capable of generating complex and beautiful patterns. Starting with any number, a Fibonacci series progresses by adding that number to the number immediately preceding it; the sum of these two numbers will produce the next number in the series. This number, in turn, added to the previous number will produce the next number in the sequence. For example, starting with the number one, the resulting Fibonacci series would look like this: 1, 2, 3, 5, 8, 13, 21, 34, 55, 89. . . and so on.

The Fibonacci series can be found everywhere in nature: in the seed head of a sunflower, pinecones, and the nautilus seashell. Fibonacci numbers are closely connected with the Golden Mean.

© Hadrian, 2014. Used under license with Shutterstock, Inc.

## Types of Shapes

Enclosing a continuous line, or filling the enclosed area with a color or texture, can create shape. Shapes may have defined, implied, or amorphous borders. A geometric shape is an example of a defined border. An implied shape is the suggestion of a shape that does not actually exist. An amorphous shape's border is so vague or delicate that its edges cannot be determined with any degree of exactitude.

Shapes can be regular and geometric, based on simple mathematics and created with a straight edge and compass or they can be curvilinear, organic, and freeform, with complex curves looking like those found in nature. Depending on their role in a composition, they can physically vary in size, position, balance, color, value, and texture.

Artists can make shapes appear to be static and stable, active and lively or seem to contract and expand. They can be realistic and instantly recognizable, or abstract and non-representational. They can be unnatural and distorted or polished and idealized. How the shape appears physically determines its character and defines it.

### Geometric and Rectangular Shapes

Geometric shapes are identified by their distinguishable crisp, precise, angular edges, and mathematically consistent curves. Although they do appear in nature as crystalline structures and growth patterns, they are usually associated with the technological world of architecture and industry.

The most familiar geometric shapes are circles, squares, rectangles, triangles, and so on. Geometric shapes are visually familiar and viewers tend to readily respond to these shapes. An artist can take advantage of this familiarity, but has to assume that viewers have preconceived notions about these shapes. A viewer tends to visually perceive that a circle will roll and that a triangle is stable, provided its base is parallel to the bottom of the picture frame.

Rectilinear shapes are geometric shapes. They consist entirely of straight lines that usually run parallel to the horizontal and vertical planes.

### Biomorphic and Curvilinear Shapes

A biomorphic shape is a nonrepresentational shape that bases artistic design elements on naturally occurring patterns or shapes reminiscent of nature. They are irregular, rounded, blobby shapes that appear to freely and at times gracefully develop. Biomorphic shapes are rounded and irregular, unlike the hard-lined straight edges found in most geometric shapes.

Like biomorphic shapes, organic shapes found in nature influence curvilinear shapes. They are rounded and curved shapes that are graceful, supple, twisting, winding, and flowing.

## Abstract

Most people use the word abstract improperly. It is not something out of the imagination of the artist that has no basis in reality. In fact, reality is the starting point of abstraction. In art, to abstract means to simplify an object down to its essential basics, its essence. Abstraction is the removal of details as the shapes are reduced to their simplest states. All forms, no matter how complex, can be essentially based on and reduced to primitive geometric shapes. When shapes are simplified to their simplest states, it is called reduction.

Abstraction has been around for centuries and the term is mostly applied to works that are simplified and visually reduced to basic elements on the picture plane. An artist will abstract a design just because of his love and appreciation of shapes and his delight in finding simplicity. The simplification of a design is the main concept of the design principle "economy."

## Nonobjective

Abstract shapes are referred to as nonobjective. A nonobjective shape is one that is not derived from an observable object or that does not physically exist. If the object of a painting is purely contrived by the imagination of the artist and has no object reference or basis in reality, then the shape is termed nonobjective, subjective, or nonrepresentational. Since no viewer has any past experience with them, invented shapes can be used more freely than geometric shapes and without the suggestion of subject matter.

## Objective

When a shape represents or resembles an actual object, it is called objective. It can also be referred to as naturalistic, representational, or realistic. Objective representation is most often used in drawing.

## Naturalism

Naturalism is synonymous with realism and tends to be how the general population judges the success of an artwork and the skill level of the artist. Though both judgments can be accurate, this does not guarantee that the artwork is a successful design.

In naturalism, the artist skillfully documents a visual image paying careful attention to represent the correct proportions, perspective, and values in an attempt to create the illusion of volume and ensure that the object occupies three-dimensional space. With naturalism, the goal is to create a sense of credibility, reality, and believability.

## Exaggerated Shapes

Distortion or exaggerated shapes are familiar to us through caricatures and even the playful effects possible on your laptop's camera. Here shapes are stretched and their proportions altered. Distortion disregards the shapes and forms of nature and purposely exaggerates the characteristics of the subject. An artist may use distortion as a means to emphasize design elements as well as develop the composition's expressive qualities. This type of shape is intended to provoke and evoke an emotional response from the viewer in a form of art often called expressionism.

## Idealism

As presented above, naturalism focuses on appearance. Its goal is to develop the shape as accurately as visually possible. Similar to this is idealism. With idealism, reality still exists, but it is "perfected." Idealism reproduces the world not as it really exists, but as an artist thinks it should look. These forms are based upon artificial standards of perfection with all the flaws, accidents, and incongruities of the visual world corrected.

# ASSIGNMENT 3.11

In your sketchbook, create designs using the element "shape," that reflect the following emotions: anxiety, hope, fear, submissive, and contemplation.

# Positive and Negative Shapes in the Composition

The figure or field is the shape that has been placed on to the background. It may also be referred to as the positive area. In the example image above, the dog would be considered the figure or positive area on the picture plane. The white area surrounding the dog is considered the ground. The ground area of a design is the unoccupied or relatively unimportant space in the picture, also known as the negative shape.

A composition begins the moment an artist places a mark on the paper. This mark, now considered the positive area, defines the remaining space as the ground or the negative space. The positive area of a composition generally will be smaller and appear to be physically in front of the ground. Adding more positive shapes to the ground causes a change to occur. As the positive shapes fill the picture plane, the ground area is reduced. The figure and the ground have an active relationship. As the space that the figure occupies increases, the ground shrinks, but its contribution to the composition increases because the negative space becomes more defined and has more visual presence.

As an artist develops his composition, he needs to consider the relationship between the negative and the positive shapes. Its success will depend on the artist's ensuring that both the positive and the negative shapes actively contribute equally to the overall composition. If the negative areas are made more interesting, the positive–negative integration improves.

When it is not apparent which shape is the figure or the ground and the viewer's attention is made to flip back and forth between them, the design is considered to have equivocal space. If handled successfully, these ambiguities will tease viewers and entice their interest in the composition.

Although artistic approaches, themes, and purposes vary, integration between the figure–ground relationships still must be developed. In representational compositions, the figure–ground relationship is usually quite clear. The subject is the focal point, but the negative is equally important in the final composition. Creating a balanced figure–ground relationship is pertinent to the success of the design.

# ASSIGNMENT 3.12

In your sketchbook, create a design in which both the positive and negative shapes contribute equally to the composition. Make two copies and in the first one, fill the in the positive area with ink. In the second copy fill in only the ground area of the design with ink. Ensure that both compositions reflect a strong understanding of the principles of organization.

## Use of Shapes

Within the composition, shapes have several roles. An artist chooses a shape to suggest an actual or invented object. Whatever type of shape the artist chooses, the shape needs to be contextually integrated with the artist's idea or intent. Physically the shapes are manipulated to develop a sense of depth or space on the picture plane and suggest mass and volume. Using the principles of organization as guides, the shapes are placed within the composition to achieve a sense of visual unity. An artist is constantly exploring and evaluating the relationship between harmony and variety. Finally, shapes serve as key visual points that determine the viewer's time spent looking at an artwork, the rhythm in which the viewer explores it, and the visual pathway she follows while looking at the composition.

# ASSIGNMENT 3.13

Photocopy a composition and overlay a sheet of tracing paper on top of it. Using arrows, reproduce the pathways your eyes take while discovering the artwork. Indicate resting points or pauses you make with solid circles. Insert these pages into your sketchbook and label them accordingly.

# Shape Dimensions

Shapes can be used to develop and represent a sense of space or depth of field within the picture plane. A shape can be perceived as two-dimensionally flat or developed as a three-dimensional illusion of mass. Arranging two or more flat or curvilinear planes, in relation to one another, gives them an appearance of solidity and produces the illusion of mass or volume. Using perspective to assist with the alignment of these shapes will help keep the illusion believable.

The picture plane is the first shape an artist needs to be aware of. For most compositions, this will be the rectangle. The orientation of the rectangle, whether vertical (portrait) or horizontal (landscape), is the first consideration in implementing the artist's concept.

An artist can overlap, vary the color and value, as well as manipulate the texture of shapes to help develop the illusion of depth or space within the picture plane.

A shape's function within a composition is complex. In order to facilitate these functions, an artist can follow proven guidelines called principles of organization. An artist's first encounter with shape begins with her deciding the orientation of the picture plane. Shapes represent the artist's idea, visually balance the composition, define harmony and variety, develop the illusion of space, control the viewer, and ensure that the artist's idea is depicted. This is why they are considered the building blocks of a composition.

# Shape and Compositional Balance

Balance is defined as a sense of equilibrium achieved through implied weight, maintaining a viewer's attention, or by manipulating the visual elements within an artwork in order to accomplish unity. Shape is instrumental in creating balance.

Like all of the other elements, shape has certain variables artists will manipulate until they determine the proper tension or directional forces within their composition such as: placement, size, visual complexity, value, texture, and color.

## Placement and Size

The physical placement and size of shape in regards to the fulcrum of the composition greatly affects the balance of a composition. A larger shape placed in the center of a composition has less visual weight than if it were placed closer to the edge of the picture plane. The same is true with a smaller shape. The further away it is from the fulcrum of the page, the more visual weight it possesses.

## Visual Complexity

A more complex, unusual, and unrecognizable shape possesses more visual complexity than a simple, common, and recognizable one. When viewers see something they do not recognize or that is a complex shape, they will spend more time looking at it while their mind attempts to make sense of what they are seeing.

© OLEKSANDR ROZDOBUDKO, 2014. Used under license with Shutterstock, Inc.

## Value

When using the value of a shape to balance a composition, it is more important to consider the shape's level of contrast to the background. A small shape that has a high contrast to its background will have more visual weight and be able to balance a larger shape on a low contrasting background.

© Rebecca J. Lansdown, 2014. Used under license with Shutterstock, Inc.

## Texture

Since texture has variegated dark and light patterns, it holds more interest for the viewer than a smooth, unrelieved surface. This can be explained by applying what we have learned about visual complexity and value. A texture is a complex visual or actual surface and commands more of the viewer's attention. Since most textures are defined by contrasting value patterns, we can say that textured shapes attract more attention than shapes lacking contrasting patterns. In review, a small rich textured shape will command more attention than a larger shape with a neutral surface.

© man_kukuku, 2014. Used under license with Shutterstock, Inc.

## Color

Color is important to shape and balance. Most individuals are more attracted to color than to black and white. Color introduced to a black and white composition will command attention to itself. In this sense, color functions a lot like value when it comes to balancing an artwork. The brighter the color contrast against the background, the more visual weight the shape will command. A small shape of color with a high contrasting background will balance a larger shape of color with low contrasting background.

© Sukharevskyy Dmytro (nevodka), 2014. Used under license with Shutterstock, Inc.

# ASSIGNMENT 3.14

In your sketchbook, create two different balanced compositions using shape for each of the following concepts: placement, size, visual complexity, value, texture, and color. Label them accordingly.

# Eye Direction/Pathways

An artist plans visual pathways into the composition to control the viewer's experience. These paths ensure the proper sequence, order of importance, and cadence in which the viewer experiences the shapes in a composition. Most of the time, these visual pathways are the result of the direction, alignment, and placement of shapes on the picture plane or in conjunction with the other art elements.

One way to create pathways for the viewer is to control the shape's direction. If shapes all point in a specific direction, they will tend to unify themselves and produce a visual path for the viewer. The second way is to align the shapes through visual linking or grouping concepts. With this technique, paths created using alignment are placed in such a manner so that their outer edges align and the viewer's eye easily moves from one shape to another in a certain direction. A third solution involves intuitive space and relies on the viewer's experiences. Here the shapes are arranged in an implied perspective that suggests the shapes exist in space. The placement of shapes creates pathways that activate and develop the picture plane three-dimensionally.

Pathways are devised to encourage transition from one pictorial area to another. When these paths are easy continuous paths, they instill a sense of peacefulness and relaxation. When the pathways are short and broken, the viewer gets the opposite effect and feels uneasy and frustrated. An artist who understands pathways and controls the viewer's experience strengthens the impact of her work. Generally, the visual paths of an artwork are rhythmic and produce a positive experience for the viewer as well as a unified composition. The direction of our eyes along these paths should be rhythmic, pleasing, informative, and help unify the design. Paths should tell the same story as the subject matter or theme and support the psychological and emotional intent of the artwork.

## Duration and Relative Dominance

© lendy16, 2014. Used under license with Shutterstock, Inc.

Pathways, duration, and dominance all work in unison to tell the artist's story. A pathway takes the viewer on a unifying and rhythmic visual journey of discovery. It defines the route of discovery and duration determines the number and length of pauses the eye takes while on that journey. The viewer's experience will be more monotonous if the pauses are of equal duration and presented in a constant rhythm. If the pauses vary a little, but not too much, the viewer's experience will be a bit more invigorating. The length of these pauses should reflect the hierarchy of the shape's importance to conveying the artist's narrative.

Although shapes can create visual pathways, they are very often focal points in a picture. Shapes can be manipulated by size, value, location, color, or any combination of these elements to achieve dominance. The principle device used to create dominance is increasing the shape's size.

Once an artist decides what area will be dominant or emphasized, he begins a dialogue with the artwork that involves reconciling the demand that dominance places on the other design principles. In general, the more dominant a shape is, the more important it tends to be to the composition, as well as to the artist. In both representational and abstract artworks, artists use a visual hierarchy system that includes both dominant and subordinate components. The artist strives to construct visual pathways in which viewers spend more time observing dominant components of a design and less time on subordinate items.

# ASSIGNMENT 3.15

In your sketchbook, design four separate compositions in which shapes are used to move the viewer throughout the artwork at different speeds. One composition should be fast, another slow, the third, a mixture of fast to slow movement, and finally the fourth, a slow to fast pace. Each composition needs to control the viewer's visual experience, utilize the entire picture plane, present unique pathways to at least five focal points of interest, and present a perceived visual hierarchy within the points of interest.

# Harmony and Variety of Shape

Harmony is the principle that ensures that everything appears unified. Shape, along with the other elements of art, achieves this goal through repetition. In art, repeating a shape's color, texture, size, or the actual shape helps ensure a sense of unity. The repeated elements need not be exactly the same, but similar enough to give the viewer a sense of familiarity. To avoid boredom, an artist has to be careful not to develop a composition where harmony exists without variety.

The principle concept of variety is the complement of harmony. An artist may introduce variety of shapes or their properties to bring enough difference to a harmonized design to enliven or draw attention to the uniformity. These differences in shape grasp and hold the viewer's attention for the period thought necessary by the artist. Successful compositions strike a balance between the comfort and security of repeated shapes or their properties and the anxiety and agitation induced by the lack of expected repetition.

Although the presence of some differences is essential, excessive differences disrupt the design unity and agitate the viewer. A good guide to remember is that repetitive shapes produce harmony and contrasting shapes introduce variety.

# Shapes and Space

Even though the manner in which space has been defined has varied historically and culturally, shapes have remained an important element to defining it. In two-dimensional design, space is limited to the picture plane and whatever illusion the artist can create on it. The picture plane is the virtual space within the picture frame. It defines the working area of the composition on which shapes are positioned and orientated.

In two-dimensional art, a shape creates the illusion of space. To create a sense of depth, artists may vary a shape's size, overlap shapes, change their vertical location, place them according to aerial perspective, vary their shading, or create an open or closed compositional structure to help two-dimensional shapes produce the illusion of space. As a rule, objects that are placed lower on the picture plane are perceived to be closer to us and high on the picture plane, to be further away.

Another way of defining space on the picture plane is by using perspective. The rules of perspective are especially effective in developing the illusion of space with shapes and dictate how a shape is oriented and placed on the picture plane; this concept will be further discussed in the chapter on space. In a perspective drawing, a larger item is also perceived to be closer to the viewer than a smaller one. This creates a more believable suggestion of space when size is coupled with overlapping and shading.

When shapes overlap on the page, the shape that maintains its features is perceived to be in front of the other. An artist will often use shading to clearly define the positioning of shapes in relation to each other and to position them in space. According to atmospheric perspective, a shape or the part of it that is closer to us will be truer in hue, higher in contrast, and more clearly defined. Objects that are in the distance will be grayer in color, lower in contrast, and have fewer details.

A shape can be further developed as a form by adding shading. Using shading, the artist creates the illusion of different depths of field. The lighter area of a shape will be perceived as advancing toward the viewer and dark values receding. The speed in which the light to dark transition occurs defines the sharpness of an angle or the radius of a curve. A faster transition from light to dark would imply a sharper angle or tighter radius.

# Shape and Content

The visual arts are about communicating through the manipulation of the art elements. In the visual arts, shapes play an important part in achieving this goal.

During the 20th century, the use of shape in a nonrepresentational manner influenced complete movements from the abstract art of the early 1900s to the conceptual movement of the seventies and eighties.

Artists use shapes to visually present their ideas. Each shape has character that distinguishes it from other shapes. Reconfiguring a shape physically changes the shape's content and expressive meaning. Artists manipulate shapes physically till shapes properly express the artists' ideas. A shape's extremities are important. They define the shape and distinguish it from its surroundings. A soft-edge shape may feel more integrated with its background thus forming a more comfortable relationship. A hard-edge shape has very defined borders that completely separate it from the background or surrounding shapes and conveys a sense of separation and individuality to the viewer. Color, value, texture, and different media all help further define and differentiate the expressive qualities of a shape and how the viewer perceives them.

Artists will select shapes to express an idea, but they may initially also be motivated by the psychological associations of shape. The best way to understand the psychological meaning of a shape is to describe it physically or use it as an adjective in a sentence. As an example, a square shape will suggest stability, perfection, solidity, symmetry, self-reliance, and predictability; whereas a circle conjures up psychological thoughts of self-possession, independence, nature, confinement, creation, or instability.

There is a close relationship between shapes and psychology. Shapes can provoke powerful emotional responses on different levels. This powerful relationship is confirmed by the use of the Rorschach test. A Rorschach test is a psychological tool designed to aid in evaluating the emotional stability of patients. The subjects' perceptions of inkblots are recorded and then analyzed using psychological interpretations, complex algorithms, or both. The images themselves are only one component of the test, whose focus is the analysis of the perception of the images.

For an artist, understanding shape is a lifelong endeavor, because the qualities of expression, or character, provided by shapes in a work of art are infinite.

# ASSIGNMENT 3.16

In your sketchbook, create a work of art in which the message or intent is conveyed through ten individual steps that illustrate the transformation of one recognizable object to another recognizable object. Each successive shape should physically relate to the previous step.

# VALUE

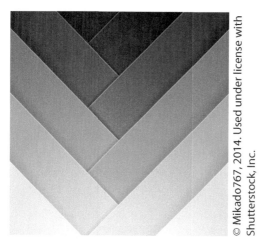

In art and design, value refers to the lightness and darkness of a surface. There is a spectrum of lights and darks, ranging from pure white to dark black, including the grays in between. White under brilliant illumination is the lightest possible value and black in shadow the darkest. Pure black, white, and gray seldom occur in the natural world for almost every surface has some local coloration, which in turn is influenced by the color of the source of illumination. Every surface, however, no matter what its color, possesses a relative degree of lightness or darkness that the artist can analyze and record as value.

Value is one of the main attributes of color. It refers to the characteristic of color determined by light or dark, or the quantity of light reflected by the color. If we add black to a color, we will get a shade. When we add white to a color, it is called a tint. Values can be discussed as high- and low-key values. Low-key values range from mid-value gray to black and high-key values range from mid-gray to white. The actual coloration of the subject, its lightness or darkness relative to its surroundings, and the degree to which the subject is illuminated or in shadow all affect our perception of value.

Value can be discussed by itself or in conjunction with color. Because color is such a complex and vast topic, it has its own dedicated chapter. In this section, we will discuss achromatic values. An achromatic value includes the limitless grays that can be made from mixing only white and black without the addition of color.

The average person can discern up to 40 variations in value. When there are more, we see a continuous graduation. Our ability to see contrast is important in identifying shapes. Our perception of a value of gray-scale (and color) is influenced by the values surrounding it. A gray square on a white surface appears heavy and imposing. The same gray square has less visual weight and seems luminous when a black background surrounds it.

## How Vision Works

The human eye contains two types of sensors: rods and cones. Both rods and cones enable us to see value. Cones are sensitive to bright lights and enable us to see and differentiate between hues. Rods, which are more numerous, are sensitive to dim light and help us see at night. In reduced light, our visual perception is more dependent on value contrast than on color.

Value can be used to help make a two-dimensional shape appear three-dimensional, move a viewer through a composition, create balance, create focal points, suggest space, and change how we perceive color.

## Values and Rendering Three-Dimensional Objects

The most important skill you need to develop to be able to draw is your ability to "see." Paying attention to a still life composition is not natural and the hardest part is convincing your mind to be attentive. Direct observation of a still life with careful attention to the relationships between shadows and shapes will help you see and understand how to create three-dimensional space on a two-dimensional plane using value. One of the most important lessons a young artist must learn is how value works to develop a shape into a mass.

The best way to grasp an understanding of value is to make value scales. You will gain experience and insight mixing the new medium and see the range of values it is capable of producing. In general, lighter values will move forward and darker values recede. The surface topography of the object being rendered will determine the speed of this transition from one value to another.

# ASSIGNMENT 3.17

Create a 10-step achromatic value scale by mixing only white and black paints together. Each value step is to be composed on a 1" x 1 1/2" painted rectangle and glued down in a linear arrangement in your sketchbook. Make sure each value step is clearly defined and they progress evenly from white to black across all 10 steps.

## Perception of Value

There are three factors influencing our perception of value: its actual coloration, the lighting of the subject, and its lightness or darkness relative to its surroundings.

The apparent value of an area is relative to the value that surrounds it. Rather than being influenced by the local value, an artist must learn to see value relationships. Local value in drawing or painting refers to the essential value of an object's or figure's surface without the inclusion of any texture or lighting. Local value is the value of an object or figure without any shadow pattern. The ability to see values accurately only comes with experience.

## Value in Drawings

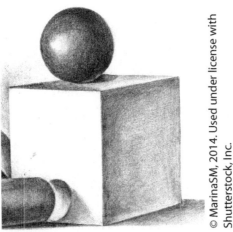

© MarinaSM, 2014. Used under license with Shutterstock, Inc.

As mentioned previously, you learn to draw by learning to see. Learning to see means developing an understanding of values through careful and direct observation and analyzing how light envelops the mass of an object. The object's three-dimensional mass will affect and alter the distribution of light and shade. Every object has a specific three-dimensional character that constitutes its mass.

We recognize the objects in the image above because of the unique way they are defined by light and shadows. The orientation of the light source determines what proportion of an object receives light and which surface is cast in a shadow. Surfaces at a right angle to the source of light will receive the most light. In the image above, this would be the left side of the cube and white area of the sphere. Areas that turn away from the light and are hidden from direct rays of light will fall into a shadow. These areas might possibly receive a softer reflected light from neighboring objects or surfaces. A cast shadow is projected from an illuminated form onto other objects or the background. A core shadow is the darkest part of the cast shadow. It is attached to the object or mass casting the shadow. In the image above, the core shadow is represented by the darkest value located to the right of where the sphere meets the top of the cube. Cast and core shadows must be considered as contributing to the overall composition.

Light does not stop dead when it hits a surface, but bounces around the scene, diminishing in strength as it goes. Even the side of an object hidden from the light source will receive some degree of illumination from light reflected and retransmitted from other objects nearby. A highlight has the highest value on a modeled form. It can be a distinct dot or areas on the surface of a shiny form that accentuates its glossiness. The lightest value on the sphere and the lightest value on the cylinder are highlights.

An artist will move a viewer through a composition by developing focal points. Often the artist will use areas of contrasting values to attract the viewer's eye to that part of the picture. Varying the size of the area and the degree of contrast will develop differing degrees of importance and a sense of hierarchy within the composition.

# ASSIGNMENT 3.18

Make a photocopy of a composition that has a pronounced light source and cast shadows. Overlay a sheet of tracing paper on top of it, then identify, trace, and label as many of the values as possible. Insert these pages into your sketchbook and label them accordingly.

© Phant, 2014. Used under license with Shutterstock, Inc.

© Phant, 2014. Used under license with Shutterstock, Inc.

# Value Patterns

Value pattern is the amount of value variation, independent of color, used to create the underlying movement or ground system of a composition. To see the value pattern of a composition, squint your eyes and look at it. This will reduce the composition down to its basic essentials: no details, no color, and no subject matter, just light and dark shapes.

When successfully integrated into an artwork, value patterns add movement, tension, and structure and reinforce the subject. They should not distract or separate themselves as overpowering entities or isolated components.

An artist uses small and undeveloped thumbnail drawings to experiment with and resolve the value patterns of her composition. These monochromatic line and wash drawings enable the artist to quickly establish rhythms and ambiguous shapes, alter the composition, establish the mood, and ensure the underlying structure is integrated into the artwork.

# ASSIGNMENT 3.19

Photocopy a composition and overlay a sheet of tracing paper on top of it. Squint and identify the major shapes that form the composition. With an ink wash, identify these shapes that indicate the underlying structure of a composition. On a separate sheet of paper, describe in writing how the structure complements or contradicts the subject matter of the composition. Insert these pages into your sketchbook and label them accordingly.

## Components of Value

The two main components of value that develop emotion and enable us to see a shape are contrast and tonal range.

### Contrast

Value contrast refers to the value difference between adjacent areas and is pertinent to the legibility of a shape. Since black and white are at the opposite ends of the achromatic scale, they have a high contrast and high visibility when placed next to one another. The lower the contrast between adjacent shapes, the less visibility they tend to have. These value relationships are exploited to develop areas of emphasis and to guide the viewer through a composition.

### Tonal Range

The second component of value is tonal range. Tonal range is the various shades of gray between absolute black and absolute white. In an art composition, it is used to establish the mood or emotion in an artwork. A tonal range consisting of black to mid-tones is called low key and can create an air of mystery, seriousness, or doom. A high-key tonal range, consisting of mid-tones to white is understated, calm, and tranquil and emits a sense of lightness and positivity to the atmosphere of the picture.

## Value Techniques

### Chiaroscuro

© Dragos Pop, 2014. Used under license with Shutterstock, Inc.

Chiaroscuro is the Italian term that translates literally into light-dark. It comes from the Italian chiaro ("clear" or "light") and oscuro ("obscure" or "dark") and refers to distribution of light and dark values to imply depth and volume in a painting or drawing.

Chiaroscuro is used to describe more dramatic and theatrical compositions that use high contrasting light and dark values.

As an art technique, chiaroscuro means to render an object using a continuous gradation of value to create the illusion of three-dimensional forms in two-dimensional artworks. The principle behind chiaroscuro is to leave the light parts as they are, so that they can be seen clearly, and to darken the "obscure" parts—the areas the artist deems less important—so that they do not distract the viewer.

# Sfumato

© murengstockphoto, 2014. Used under license with Shutterstock, Inc.

Sfumato is the Italian word meaning smoke. Sfumato is a subtle shading technique, which describes a transition of tone from light to dark that is so gradual that the eye cannot detect any distinct tones or boundaries between values. Leonardo da Vinci described Sfumato as a technique of merging a light value to a darker shade without the evidence of lines or borders. The transition from one value to another should be indiscernible, like smoke.

# Tenebrism

© Antonov Roman, 2014. Used under license with Shutterstock, Inc.

Tenebrism comes from the Italian word tenebroso, meaning "obscure." Tenebrism is a style of chiaroscuro painting in which the artists were interested in the peculiarities of lighting, particularly the way that lighting affected mood and emotional expression. They deviated from standard light conditions by placing the implied light sources in unexpected locations, creating unusual visual and spatial effects. It is the more violent style of chiaroscuro painting.

# Value and Space

The development of volume and space are the most important uses of value gradations in art. An artwork that lacks much of a value range tends to appear flat and suggest a shallow depth of field. Within a composition, space is considered the negative or ground area and the complement to a figure or form. Artists not only use value to define a form, they use it to place that form in space as well.

As described earlier, in an atmospheric perspective, areas of high contrasting values will pull forward and low contrasting values will recede. Both white and black can be pushed forward or back in space, depending on other spatial clues given: overlapping, sharper details, or value contrasts. Within the picture plane, there is a limited achromatic range of values that can actually be used. This limited range of values is referred to as the dynamic range of value. Artists may use both black and white to represent objects seen in the near distance, but only gray will recede into the far distance.

## Creating a Focal Point

Value is pertinent to balancing a composition and conveying the artist's intent. Knowing how to use value to develop focal points, or emphasis, is an invaluable tool for the artist. Strong contrasts of light and dark, along with linear movements, create focal points that can direct the viewer's attention to parts of the composition according to their relative significance. High contrast between dark and light instantly attracts our attention because of value emphasis. By planning high contrast in one area and subdued contrasts elsewhere, the artist can ensure where the viewer's eye will be directed first. Emphasis, through dramatic value contrasts, works equally well whether a composition is representational or abstract.

## Physical and Psychological Space

Value distribution refers to the proportion and arrangement of lights and darks in balancing a composition and directly affects both the emotional and physical components of an artwork.

Emotional balance is when an artist pays particular attention to the value range and contrast while creating a unified composition. Careful use of the value distribution can increase emotional impact. A composition that has a higher percentage of dark values will create a sense of mystery or increased dramatic tension. A composition with a higher percentage of white values will suggest openness, optimism, and clarity.

Throughout this chapter, we have presented ways that values have been used to solicit intended emotional responses from a viewer. As we mentioned at the end of the chapter on line, the emotional response viewers have to a work of art is complicated and determined by their personal experiences. There are no absolute rules in art. With value, some basic tenets are that strong value contrasts tend to provoke an immediate emotional response. A dark background with light images can evoke a sense of fear, like dreadful dreams in darkness. Use of many dark areas in a work can also set a bleak, lonely mood. Although black is often associated with somberness, this is not always the case. Sometimes, black is used to evoke a feeling of sensual warmth. A range of mid-values that cannot be mistaken for blacks or whites can convey a sense of hopelessness or depression. Even in abstractions, in which there is no recognizable image to influence our emotional responses, values can affect us strongly.

Value assumes a dominant role in determining the mood of an artwork. A work that exploits full contrast of value conveys a feeling of aliveness and vigor. Compositions in which close value relationships dominate, while contrasts are minimized, may create a sense of quiet and soothing restfulness or of introspection and brooding subjectivity. Predominantly light compositions carry a sense of illumination, clarity, and perhaps a rational, optimistic outlook. On the other hand, compositions predominantly dark in value often suggest night, darkness, mystery, and fear. Dark on dark values with little to no contrast equals troubled psychological space, while high-value contrast suggests a happier and stimulating psychological response.

As previously mentioned, artists use thumbnail sketches to explore the light and dark value patterns and to create a structural framework upon which to build the tone of their composition. Artists base their compositional decisions on the art elements and principles of organization, not on the laws of nature, to develop a unified artwork.

An artist chooses a value range based on the mood and expressive character he wishes to convey to the viewer. The terms high key, middle key, low key, and full range are used to describe the general tonality of two-dimensional artworks.

Value ranges are identified and named based on their limited number of closely related values. High key refers to the light values—white through middle gray on the value scale—where the darkest value is no darker than middle gray. Middle-key compositions include the five values in the middle of the scale between light and dark. Low-key values refer to the dark half of the value scale-middle gray to black. It is the overall tonality that determines the key of any drawing.

A composition with a full range of values is one that uses the complete achromatic value range. A full range of value does not imply that all are used equally throughout the composition. While developing an artwork, it is important to determine the lightest and darkest value possible from the medium or media you have chosen in order to determine your potential range of values.

# ASSIGNMENT 3.20

Make a black and white photocopy of a colored composition. Analyze it and in writing describe how the subject matter and the range of values complement each other to produce a unified narrative or do not complement each other and produce a disjointed narrative. Insert these pages into your sketchbook.

## Experimenting with Technique

Each medium and technique of application has a unique expressive quality. The need to experiment with and gain a working knowledge of a variety of media and how they might be applied is extremely important. It is through these experiences that an artist develops a visual vocabulary and an understanding of the contextual integration between an idea and materials.

## Open and Closed-Value Patterns

When strongly aligned with composition, value becomes a powerful communicative tool. A value pattern can be developed in two ways: open and closed. The difference between the two is whether or not the edges or boundaries of the shapes limit or do not contain the values of the composition. With closed-value compositions, both objects and values are limited and isolated by the edges of the shapes. In open-value compositions, values can cross over shape boundaries into adjoining areas, helping integrate and unify the composition.

The potential for emotional expression through the combination of open and closed values is endless. The artist may choose a closely related value scheme for hazy, fog-like effects or a sharply defined value scheme for dramatic contrasting effects. These schemes may be purely decorative or be over-the-top expressive. They are multipurpose tools, and the success of the total work of art is based largely on the effectiveness with which the artist has controlled the expressive language of value.

## Relationship Between Value and Color

As mentioned in the beginning of this chapter, value and color are closely related to each other. In some respects, they are inseparable; every hue is inherent with a value. Pure yellow is a light (high-value) color corresponding to a very light gray in terms of light reflection. Purple is basically a dark (low-value) color that would match a very dark gray. A pure red will fall in the middle of the value scale.

These relationships will be further explored in the chapter on color.

## Compositional Function of Value

In this chapter, we covered value as an important art element that enables artists to develop a shape into a three-dimensional form—that it can be used to determine the placement and relationship of a form in space on the picture plane. We learned that value could suggest a texture on the surface of an object and how to use value in a composition to develop emotions. Finally, we learned that value could develop focal points to move a viewer around a composition and to define a hierarchy of importance.

The contribution and importance of the art element, value, is immense. It is a vital and a lively participant in the composition. An artist strengthens underlying compositional structure by controlling the contrast of value. Value is instrumental in creating relative dominance, depicting two-dimensional patterns, establishing mood, and producing spatial unity. Understanding how it functions and its potential contribution to visual language is invaluable to the artist, especially one just starting her career.

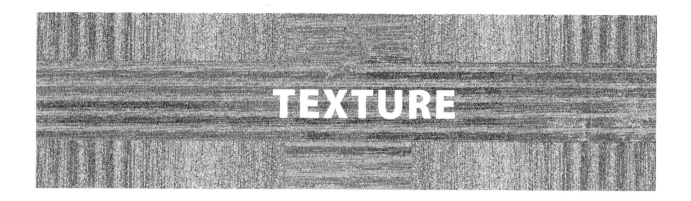

# Texture

In everyday speech, texture means sensations we understand through touch. In this textbook, texture refers to the surface character of a material that can be experienced through touch or the illusion of touch. It can be made by natural forces or through the artistic manipulation of the art elements to embellish the surfaces of two-dimensional shapes and three-dimensional volumes. Texture is unique among the elements because it engages two senses: our sense of touch as well as our vision.

Artists use texture to enhance the visual surface and develop the conceptual intent of their design. Although texture is more intimately and dramatically known through the sense of touch, we can see texture and thus, indirectly, predict how it would feel.

Everything has an actual texture or textural effect that is interpreted visually. Since every work of art has a surface of some sort, texture is an element in every design. In works of art, the manipulation of the textural treatment is the element we often notice first. In the following section, we will discuss four approaches to creating and using texture: actual, simulated, abstract, and invented.

## Types of Texture

### Actual Texture

The way a surface of an object looks and feels is referred to as actual texture. It is the physical surface variations that we can experience through our sense of touch. In the visual arts, it is the surface characteristics of the materials or the result of how the artist applied them. Independently, actual textures can create stunning compositions. When actual texture is used to express a specific subject matter, the artwork will be stronger if the two are congruent.

Although some textures are more pronounced than others, every medium has a texture, whether it is imbued in the medium itself or through its application. In painting, an artist may create a thick layer of paint with a trowel or work as minimally as simply staining the canvas. In both cases, the artist must be attentive to physical attributes of the texture she creates, either intentionally or unintentionally, and ensure that it is congruent with her idea.

Papier collé means "glued paper" in French. In 1908, Pablo Picasso pasted a piece of paper onto a drawing. This is the first known example of papier collé, a kind of collage in which the pasted objects are grouped for pattern rather than for symbolism. In the beginning of the 20th century, Pablo Picasso and Georges Braque are credited with introducing to the world this distinctive approach to making art. The practice of papier collé developed into collage and assemblage.

In the earlier half of the 20th century, collage became a distinctive part of modern art. Collage heightens a viewer's awareness of familiar objects by placing them in an unexpected context. As we move into the 21st century, where everything is temporary and disposable, this style of making art continues to heighten our sense of awareness.

In collage, artists can use any items they wish: tissue paper, wrapping paper, newspaper pages, magazine pages, cardboard, foil, metal, plastic, fabric, wire, photographs, found objects such as shells, feathers, stones, and 'rubbish' such as broken toys or appliances. Today, image-processing programs such as Adobe Photoshop have become another medium enabling artists to investigate the endless potential of collage. Collages remain fairly flat. When they become more three-dimensional, they are referred to as assemblages.

Assemblage is a fairly recent development. The origin of the word, in its artistic sense, can be traced back to the early 1950s, when Jean Dubuffet created a series of collages of butterfly wings, which he titled assemblages d'empreintes. However, both Marcel Duchamp and Pablo Picasso had been working with found objects for many years prior to Dubuffet.

Assemblage differs from collage in that it consists of making three-dimensional and two-dimensional compositions by putting together rather bulky individual items. Assemblages are artworks assembled from three-dimensional objects originally created for other purposes that are displayed in a variety of positions beyond but including the wall.

## Simulated Texture

© NataLT, 2014. Used under license with Shutterstock, Inc.

Simulated texture is an attempt to make a convincing copy or translation of an object's texture, in any medium, to fool the viewer. Artists focus on and attempt to reproduce every detail, surface characteristic, and identifiable feature of the object they are reproducing at such a convincing skill level that the viewer is fooled in to mistaking the objects as being real. Simulated textures are useful for making things identifiable.

A painter can create a realistic dimensional illusion of texture on a flat, smooth, painted surface. This is called verisimilitude, or an appearance that is "truly the same." By reproducing the color and value patterns of familiar textures, painters encourage us to see textures where they do not actually exist. Visual texture is the impression of texture as purely visual; it cannot be felt or enjoyed by touch. It is only suggested to our eyes. The ultimate suggestive painting in portraying visual texture is called trompe l'oeil style paintings.

Trompe-l'oeil is a French term meaning "to fool the eye" and it is commonly defined as "deceptive painting." In trompe-l'oeil paintings, the subjects are delineated with meticulous care. The artist attentively captures the exact visual colors and value patterns of each and every surface. His goal is to technically reproduce the subject matter to such a believable degree that the viewer is deceived into believing the object truly exists three-dimensionally.

Trompe l'oeil paintings works best when the composition's depth of field is shallow or as two-dimensional as possible. Because of our binocular vision, most attempts at developing a three-dimensional sense on a two-dimensional plane are thwarted.

## Abstract Texture

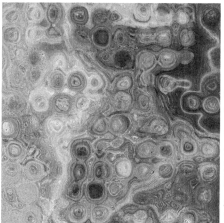

© iulias, 2014. Used under license with Shutterstock, Inc.

Similar to abstract shapes, abstract textures are natural textures that have been modified, usually in a simplified manner, to meet the needs of an artist. Within a composition, abstract textures are modified from their origin, simplified, and used more as a decorative element. In paintings, artists use abstracted textures to enrich, decorate areas, and direct the viewer's attention. There is no attempt to fool anyone, but from the context and pattern, we can recognize what the texture is meant to represent.

## Invented Texture

© iulias, 2014. Used under license with Shutterstock, Inc.

Invented textures are textures not intended to reference the objective world. They have no precedent, do not simulate an actual texture, and are not abstracted from reality. They are purely and simply created by the artist's imagination. In contemporary paintings, we often see textures that look like nothing we have seen in nature. These invented textures usually appear in abstract works, as they are entirely nonobjective and are the result of the artist's imagination.

## Creating Visual Interest

Texture functions on several levels. As an art element, it enriches the surface of a composition and unapologetically fights for the viewer's attention. It appeals to our sense of touch, thus activating more than one of our senses. And finally, our sense of vision stimulates a memory of the sensation of touch. So even if we are not able to presently touch an object, but have previously experienced such a sensation, we can vicariously experience the artwork by remembering the context of that experience. The combination of experience and memory makes texture a powerful art element.

## Texture and Composition

A viewer's attention is constantly being guided through an artwork. The degree of emphasis an artist gives an area of a composition determines the movement and direction of viewers' attention, where their eyes will rest, and which areas they will pass over or through while looking at a composition. Areas with pronounced textures will command more attention than smooth surfaces, will provide focal points for a viewer's eyes to rest, and will guide a viewer through the composition.

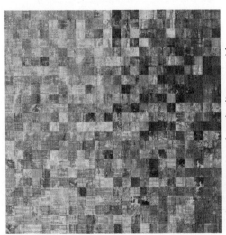

© iulias, 2014. Used under license with Shutterstock, Inc.

## Creating Texture

When an artist creates a texture, he must be conscious of three factors. First, every material has an inherent textural quality. Second, the tool he uses to apply the medium can and will affect the medium's texture. Finally, he must choose a medium and application process that develops a visual language that is congruent with his intent.

## Repetition of Art Elements

The art elements "line" or "shape" can become visual textures when they are repeated within a composition. This happens because our ability to recognize individual elements falters as they are repeatedly presented in a design. Our brain stops perceiving the individual elements and instead interprets them as an area of visual texture. This visual phenomenon is especially true if the elements are uniform, but also occurs even when they vary slightly.

## Type

Those of you who aspire to be graphic, web, or interactive designers need to realize that type creates a visual texture that is as important to design as is the legibility of the letters or numbers used. The font selection for the type, the arrangement of the text, the placement on the page, and the medium from which the subject matter is conceived make it a piece of art.

© Belinka, 2014. Used under license with Shutterstock, Inc.

## Rubbings and Transfers

Simply placing a sheet of paper over top of an object and rubbing it with a pencil or similar medium will create a texture. Texture is created by rubbing the pencil over the paper placed against the object; this produces a slightly raised surface in the paper due to the paper's surface stretching and the object's surface pattern being transferred to the paper. The pencil also produces a texture as it is rubbed against the paper and depending on the roughness of paper used, an additional texture may be produced.

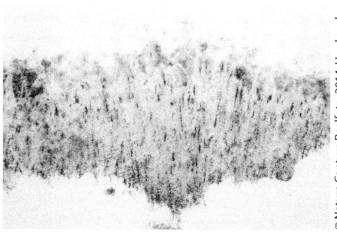

© Nature Capture Realfoto, 2014. Used under license with Shutterstock, Inc.

## Erasures

The simple act of erasing can produce amazing textures that, in the hands of an artist, can easily become the narrative or inspiration for a work of art. Through erasing, an artist can create contrast, lines, shapes, and so on. Once a mark is made with a medium, realistically you never can remove it from the page, whether it is pencil on paper or paint on canvas. The surface disruption created through the act of erasing becomes an additional texture that can become an artistic means of expression in itself.

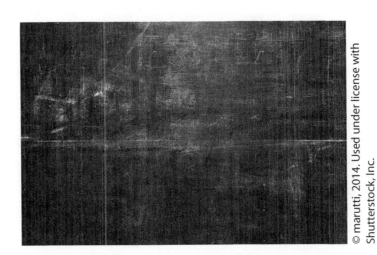

# ASSIGNMENT 3.21

In your sketchbook, create a 10-step texture value scale. Using a 4B pencil and a consistent paper selection, compile at least 10 texture rubbings. Be careful not to mark or deface public property such as walls or placards and to be consistent with the pressure you apply to your pencil. Quite often, the values of the rubbings are very similar and difficult to determine. To help you determine a value, simply squint your eyes while looking at the rubbings. If you still are unable to differentiate which value is darker, simply make a different texture lift. Cut the texture rubbing into 1" x 1 1/2" rectangles and arrange them into a linear format. Place the lightest value on the far left and the darkest value on the far right. Try to distribute the range of value as equitably as possible across the 10 rectangles and paste them into your sketchbook. When making the original texture rub, make sure they are large enough to be cut into a 1" x 1 1/2" rectangle as well as accommodate the correlating shape pattern you will need to complete assignment 3.22.

## Texture and Space

Since texture is a compilation of the other art elements, it defines space through similar principles. Whenever lines, dots, or other shapes are repeated, variations in the size, density, or orientation of these marks can be used to define different depths of field. Tightly grouped marks or a larger and thicker line will produce an area of darker value and recede. Whereas, a loosely spaced grouping or thin and smaller lines will allow more of the background to optically mix and cause the value to appear lighter. Texture's overall impact is strongest when size, density, and orientation are used in unison.

The best way to understand how texture can be manipulated to create space is to approach it from an atmospheric perspective. An atmospheric perspective represents objects as they would naturally appear to us. When working with texture from an atmospheric perspective, there are three specific components that need to be considered. First is the size of the actual texture. If a texture is larger, then it tends to move forward on the picture plane. Second is the contrast within the texture. This is the difference in value between the light and dark areas within the texture. If there is a high contrast, the texture will move forward. The lower the contrast, the more it will recede into the picture plane. The third variable that an artist needs to understand is the crispness or definition of the texture. Clearly defined textures will tend to come forward and those with blurry edges will recede.

© Slawomir Kruz, 2014. Used under license with Shutterstock, Inc.

# ASSIGNMENT 3.22

Make two black and white photocopies of a landscape that has a pronounced depth of field. Break one of the photocopies into closed value shapes. Use the texture value scale you produced in Assignment 3.21 to determine which value corresponds to each shape. Cut the textural rubbings into shapes by using the closed value shapes from the original photocopy as patterns. Keep in mind the physical nature of how textures and values create the illusion of depth. Each textural shape should be equal in value to the shape found in the original image. Using non-smudging glue, arrange and attach the cutout shapes to a white ground sheet to reproduce the original image. Make sure the cutout shapes' edges are secured and flat against the background. Insert both the original and the textural version into your sketchbook.

## Texture and Meaning

Every mark we make can add or subtract from the overall success of our design. When texture is randomly placed on the picture plane without consideration for the final design, the composition becomes cluttered and confusing to the viewer.

When an artist uses actual texture to render or paint an object, the composition is comfortable and feels right. If the same composition were created with an abstract or invented texture or one that is the complete opposite of what the viewer might think appropriate, the artist runs the risk of distancing the viewer. On the other hand, depending on what texture is paired up with the object, the viewer might be totally mesmerized. Deliberate use of texture can enhance the illusion of space and increase compositional unity.

Textures have symbolic or associative meanings and can be used as supplementary psychological devices in art. As previously mentioned, texture stimulates two senses. The more stimuli the brain receives, the better chance the artwork will provoke psychological or emotional responses within the viewer. Positive and negative experiences can equally be made through the viewer's visual associations with the environments, objects, or persons an artist might place in the composition. Textures when handled by a trained artist are powerful tools to stimulate our curiosity, shock us, or cause us to question.

## Pattern

Pattern is a design created by repeated thematic elements that are usually varied and produce interconnectedness and obvious directional movements. Although texture and pattern are very similar, the main difference between them is that texture tends to arouse the sense of touch in viewers, while pattern merely appeals to their sense of vision.

Psychologists speak of "horror vacui" or a need to fill up empty spaces, a basic human impulse. This explains a desire to add visual interest to an empty surface or space. When this surface activation is accomplished through repeated marks or shapes, we have the beginning of pattern. Pattern can be intricate or simple and is a dynamic way of capturing visual interest.

As texture becomes more and more abstracted or invented, it becomes a pattern. Although every texture makes a sort of pattern, not every pattern could be considered a texture. Pattern is mainly considered to be a two-dimensional ornamentation and not used for its three-dimensional tactile appeal like texture. As a decorative element, pattern usually involves repetition, regularity, and some symmetry. In texture, its variations usually do not involve such perfect regularity.

### Motifs in Pattern

© Goldenarts, 2014. Used under license with Shutterstock, Inc.

A motif is a recurring thematic element or repeated design feature. It may be found in both textures and patterns. When an artist emphasizes texture, a viewer is more likely to notice the surface texture before noticing the motif. The opposite is true with pattern. When an artist emphasizes pattern, viewers are more likely to see the motif and not focus on the texture of the surface.

We associate pattern with printed and woven textiles and wallpaper, which by their nature depend on repetitions, some more complicated than others. A viewer will also see the group or organization first and the individual motifs secondly. In the example above, the motif would be the individual diamond shapes created by the intersecting angular lines. Collectively, the diamond shapes create an overall pattern.

## Symmetry Patterns

Symmetrical patterns are more often used in a commercial application than in works of art. Their balanced presentation appeals to our desire to exist in a stable environment and feel comfortable psychologically. There are three ways to construct a symmetrical pattern: reflection, rotation, and translation.

### Reflection

Reflection is a symmetrical design or mirror image. If the shape were to be folded in half over the axis, the two halves would be identical: the two halves are each other's mirror image. Thus a square has four axes of symmetry, because there are four different ways to fold it and have the edges all match. A circle has infinitely many axes of symmetry, for the same reason. In 2D, there is a line of symmetry, in 3D, a plane of symmetry. An object or figure, which is indistinguishable from its transformed image, is called mirror symmetric. The pattern on butterfly wings is considered reflection symmetry.

© aidarsky, 2014. Used under license with Shutterstock, Inc.

### Rotation

Rotation symmetry is when a shape is rotated about a central point of axis. Generally speaking, an object with rotational symmetry is an object that looks the same after a certain amount of rotation. The degree of rotational symmetry is how many degrees the shape must be turned to look the same on a different side or vertex. An object may have many degrees of rotational symmetry—that is, a pattern will appear to be exactly the same several times during a single 360-degree rotation.

## Translation

Translation symmetry is when copies of the shape have been positioned horizontally, vertically, or diagonally away from the original without changing the shape. Translation means that when copies of an object are made and you shift their placement in a vertical, diagonal, or horizontal manner, they will develop into a pattern of alignment.

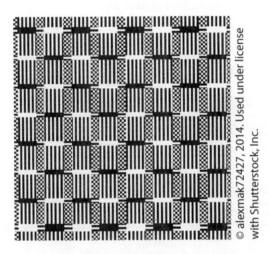

Visual impressions of what something would feel like if touched may or may not correspond to its actual surface texture. Each material has a distinctive physical texture, and each drawing method creates a distinctive visual texture. By combining physical and visual textures, we can unify a composition and add another layer of conceptual and compositional energy.

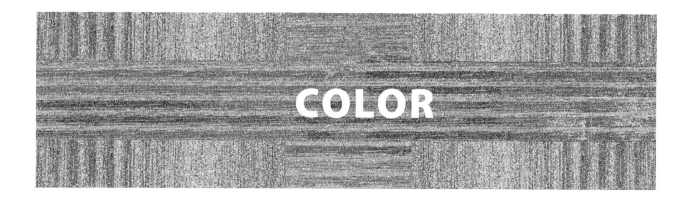

# COLOR

"Artists can color the sky red because they know it's blue. Those of us who aren't artists must color things the way they really are or people might think we're stupid."—Jules Feiffer

## Physical Properties of Color

Color is the visual response we perceive when the wavelengths of sunlight identified as red, orange, yellow, green, blue, indigo, and violet strike an object and are reflected back to our eyes.

Color is the art element to which humans are most responsive. It has a basic, instinctive visual appeal, and arouses universal appreciation. Color is one of the most expressive art elements because its quality affects our emotions directly. Although it is intimidating at times to understand, color is an amazing tool for artists. It is more complex than the other art elements. This textbook will introduce you to color theory from an artistic perspective. Reading the chapter and completing the assignments will provide you with a basic working knowledge of color from which experiential knowledge can be built.

The fundamental basis of color theory is that color only exists as a property of light, not of the object itself. Sir Isaac Newton demonstrated this property of light when in the 17th century he passed white light through a prism and the light separated into the spectrum of wavelengths visible to the human eye: red, orange, yellow, green, blue, indigo, and violet.

It is crucial in working with color to first understand that objects have no color of their own. They only have the ability to reflect certain rays of white light. White light contains the entire spectrum of color rays. Objects will absorb all of the white light rays except for the ones that their surface reflects. The color ray reflected determines the perceived color of the object. As an example, an object perceived as blue will reflect the blue light rays, but absorb all of the other ones. Objects that appear to be black absorb all of the white light rays entirely and reflect none back to the viewer. White objects appear white because they don't absorb any light rays, but instead reflect them all.

The significance of this fact for the artist is that color will change as light changes. A color will also change depending on the colors that surround it. Together, these two variables suggest that there is no one precise color of an object as defined by the wavelength of light it reflects.

Color begins with and is derived from light, either natural or artificial. Where there is little light, there is little color; where the light is strong, color is likely to be particularly intense. When the light is weak, such as at dusk or dawn, it is difficult to distinguish one color from another.

Every ray of light coming from the sun is composed of waves that vibrate at different speeds. The sensation of color is aroused in the human mind by the way our sense of vision responds to the different wavelengths.

To be able to see color, the eye needs to process wavelengths of light. Located in the retina are two kinds of receptor cells that respond to the light focused on them by the lens of the eye. These are the "rods," (so named because of their shapes), which are responsible for colorless vision in conditions of dim illumination, and the "cones" which operate at higher light levels and are responsible for color perception.

Large energies of light are required to stimulate vision on both ends of the visible band of wavelengths. However, the rods and cones of the eye are very sensitive to the wavelengths in the middle range. These wavelengths are normally seen as green and yellowish green (lime).

© Mopic, 2014. Used under license with Shutterstock, Inc.

Spectrum is a band of individual colors that appear when a beam of white light is broken into its component wavelengths, identifiable as hues. The rays of red have the longest wavelength and those of violet the shortest. The angle at which the rays are bent, or refracted, when passed through a prism, is greatest at the violet end and least at the red end.

## Color Classification

There are three principal properties to classifying color: hue, value, and intensity. These three attributes of color ultimately form a three-dimensional model or color space, which has been constructed by Munsell as a complete color reference and which will be explored more fully later in this chapter. When we refer to a color scheme, unless noted, it will be Munsell's three-dimensional color model.

### Hue

© NREY, 2014. Used under license with Shutterstock, Inc.

Although the words hue and color are often used synonymously, there is a distinction between the two terms. Hue refers specifically to the different wavelengths making up the color spectrum of light. One hue can be mixed to produce many variations of color. Even though there are relatively few hues, there can be an almost endless number of colors.

Hues are positioned, identified, and named on the 12-step color wheel. Hue designates color into distinct pure colors as determined by their wavelength. Their wavelength designates a color's position in the spectrum or on the color wheel. Hues are recognized by names such as red, orange, yellow, green, blue, indigo, and violet (ROY G BIV).

## Value

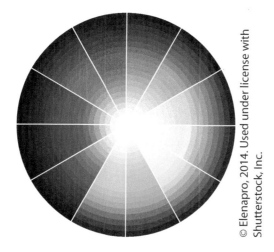

© Elenapro, 2014. Used under license with Shutterstock, Inc.

The second property of color is value. Value distinguishes between the lightness and darkness of colors, or the quantity of light a color reflects. When a hue is mixed with varying amounts of white, the colors produced are known as tints. Shades are produce when a hue is mixed with black. Value changes may also be made when we mix the pigment of one hue with the pigment of another hue that is darker or lighter; this mixing will also alter the color's hue. The only dark or light pigments available that would not also change the hue are achromatic (black, white, or gray). The addition of black, white, or gray will only change the value (the tint or shade) not the hue.

Each color reflects a different quantity of light as well as a different wavelength. A large amount of light is reflected from yellow, whereas a small amount of light is reflected from violet. Each color at its maximum intensity has a normal value that indicates the amount of light it reflects. It can, however, be made lighter or darker than normal by adding white or black, as previously noted. We should know the normal value of each of the colors in order to use them effectively. This normal value can most easily be seen when the colors of the wheel are placed next to a scale of neutral values from black to white. On this scale, all colors that are above middle gray are called high-key colors. All colors that are below middle gray are referred to as low-key colors. Whether a color remains low or high key is up to the artist. The chart below denotes a hue's gray scale brightness.

stock-vector-color-values-in-grayscale-equivalents-148889468

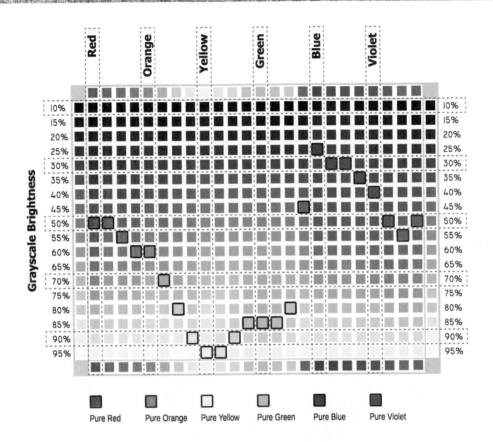

## Intensity

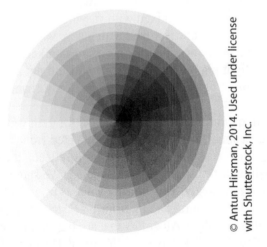

© Antun Hirsman, 2014. Used under license with Shutterstock, Inc.

The third property of color is intensity, saturation, or chroma. Intensity is the measure of the purity, brightness, or grayness of a hue in a perceived color. We use the term intensity to distinguish a brighter appearance from a duller one of the same hue, that is, to differentiate a color that has a high degree of saturation or strength from one that is grayed, neutralized, or less intense.

A saturated color is bright and intense, almost a pure hue; a unsaturated color has no hue and is called achromatic. The primary colors are the most intense. High-intensity colors are often used to maximize impact. Since a color is at full intensity only when pure and unmixed, there is a relationship between value and intensity.

Mixing black or white with a color changes its value, but at the same time, it also affects its intensity. As color loses its intensity, it tends to approach gray. A tone is a low-intensity color produced by mixing a hue with a shade of gray.

Although we cannot change value without changing intensity, we can change intensity without changing the value. As white is added to any hue, the color becomes lighter in value, but it also loses its brightness or intensity. In the same way, when black is added to a hue, the intensity diminishes as the value darkens.

# ASSIGNMENT 3.23

In your sketchbook, create three separate value scales by mixing white with red, white with yellow, and white with blue. Make sure each individual step is defined and the transition equitably distributed across 10 steps as you progress from pure white to each individual color. Each individual value scale is to be comprised of 1" x 1 1/2" painted rectangles glued down in a linear arrangement. Make sure to add the pigment to the white paint in order to control the transition and conserve your paints.

# ASSIGNMENT 3.24

In your sketchbook, create three value scales by mixing black with red, black with yellow, and black with blue. Make sure each individual step is defined and the transition equitably distributed across all 10 steps as you progress from each color to black. Each individual value scale is to be comprised of 1" x 1 1/2" painted rectangles glued down in a linear arrangement. The blue to black value scale will be the most difficult one in which to identify the individual values. It is possible, if you cautiously add the black paint in small amounts.

There are two ways to lower the intensity of a color without changing its value—that is, to make a color less bright, more neutral and dull.

By mixing the hue (pigment) with a neutral gray of the same value, one can create a variation in intensity without a change in value. The color becomes less bright as more gray is added, but it will not become lighter or darker in value.

The second and most efficient way to change the intensity of any hue is by adding the complementary hue. When mixed, complementary colors will neutralize each other until, mixed in the right proportions, they form a gray that resembles neither—represented by the gray in the center of the color wheel. These neutralized (low-intensity) versions of a color are called tones. Mixing two hues that occur exactly opposite each other on the color wheel, such as red and green, blue and orange, or yellow and violet, actually results in the intermixing of all three primaries.

Anytime complements are mixed their intensity will change, except for one pair: red-orange and blue-green. They are the only pair of complements that when mixed remain at the same intensity and at the same value level. This occurs because in theory they begin at the same value level—middle gray.

# ASSIGNMENT 3.25

In you sketchbook, create three value scales by mixing together the complements: red with green, purple with yellow, and blue with orange. Make sure each individual step is defined and the transition equitably distributed across 10 steps as you progress from one hue to its complement. Each individual value scale is to be comprised of ten 1" x 1 1/2" painted rectangles glued down in a linear arrangement. Once again, remember to add the darker pigment to the lighter one in order to control the transition and conserve your paints.

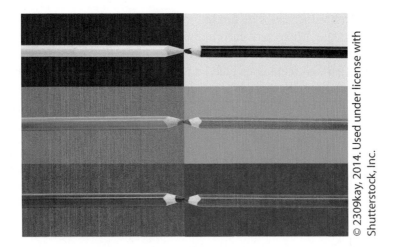

Another common approach artists use to change a color's intensity is to physically place one color next to its complement. Mixing complementary colors together dulls them, but when complementary colors are placed next to each other, they intensify each other's brightness. This effect is called simultaneous contrast, meaning that each complement simultaneously intensifies the visual brilliance of the other. Simultaneous contrast appears to increase the color's intensity. It can be explained by the one color principle that is true in all situations: colors are affected by the colors around them. Even when working with very few hues, artists can vary their effects by the ways they are combined.

## Color Systems

Although color indeed comes from light, the guidelines of color mixing and usage are different depending on whether the color source is light or pigments. Color from light combines and forms new colors based on what is called the additive system. This color system is used to create visual images on computer and television screens. On the other hand, pigments and dyes function in a subtractive system. This term is appropriate because when light hits an object's surface, the pigment absorbs (or subtracts) all of color components except for the color that is reflected to our eyes. Artists and designers use and should be aware of both additive and subtractive color systems.

It is important for an artist to be familiar with additive color systems because they are is used in video production, computer graphics, the neon sign industry, slide and multimedia presentations, laser light shows, and stage lighting. In each case, artists and technicians work with light and create color by mixing the light primaries: blue, green, and red.

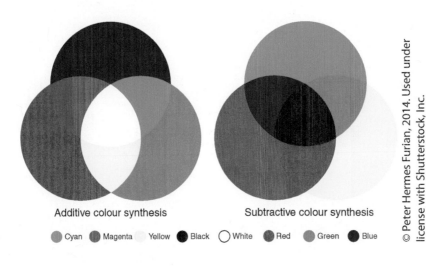

Additive colour synthesis        Subtractive colour synthesis

● Cyan  ● Magenta  ○ Yellow  ● Black  ○ White  ● Red  ● Green  ● Blue

# Additive Systems

The colors of the spectrum are pure, and they represent the greatest intensity possible. The additive primaries are red, green, and blue (RGB). When the three primaries are overlapped, they produce white light or a complete spectrum of light, thus proving that white light is the presence of all color wavelengths. Complementary or opposite hues in light—red/cyan, blue/yellow, green/magenta—when mixed will again produce white light. This happens because two complementary colors when combined encompass the entire spectrum of color. Where light from a red spotlight overlaps with light from a cyan spotlight, the visual sensation is basically white. A secondary additive color is created by mixing two primary light colors. When red and blue light overlap, magenta is produced; where red and green light overlap, yellow is produced; where green and blue light overlap, cyan is produced.

Our perception of additive color is influenced by several factors. First, the wattage or intensity of the light source for the projection may vary from incandescent or fluorescent light to daylight. Second, the overall amount of ambient light contained in the environment may vary. And finally, color is influenced by the surface on which the light is being projected. A projected light will behave differently on transparent, translucent, or textured surfaces.

The main purpose of the RGB color model is for the sensing, representing, and displaying of images in electronic systems, such as televisions and computers, though it has also been used in conventional photography. Before the electronic age, the RGB color model already had a solid theory behind it, based in human perception of colors.

RGB is a device-dependent color model: different devices detect or reproduce a given RGB value differently, since the color elements (such as phosphors or dyes) and their response to the individual R, G, and B levels vary from manufacturer to manufacturer, or even in the same device over time. Thus an RGB value does not define the same color across devices without some kind of color management.

Typical RGB input devices are color television cameras, video cameras, image scanners, and digital cameras. Typical RGB output devices are TV sets of various technologies (CRT, LCD, plasma, etc.), computer and mobile phone displays, video projectors, multicolor LED displays, and large screens such as JumboTron, and so on.

# Subtractive Systems

Any colored object has certain physical properties called color quality or pigmentation that enables it to absorb some color waves and reflect others.

Regardless of how the surface pigmentation of an object is applied or altered, the sensation of color is created when the surface absorbs all the wavelengths except those of the color perceived. When the artwork is experienced through reflected light, we are dealing with subtractive color rather than actual light rays or additive color. With an area of white, all the light wavelengths of color are reflected back to the viewer—none is subtracted by the white.

There are two categories of subtractive systems each of which has its own set of primaries. Artists who work with dyes, color printing for photography, transparent inks, and the printing industry will need to become familiar with the subtractive color primaries cyan (a deep greenish blue), magenta (a brilliant purplish pink), and yellow. Most students, on the other hand, are introduced to the subtractive primaries red, yellow, and blue which are commonly used by painters.

## Cyan, Magenta, and Yellow (CMY)

The printing industry has applied these subtractive primaries to the four-color printing process and has made great advancement in color reproduction. When the printing plates for cyan, magenta, and yellow are printed together, all the colors and value ranges possible are created.

The CMYK color model (process color, four-color) is a subtractive color model used in color printing and also used to describe the printing process itself. CMYK refers to the four inks used in some color printing: cyan, magenta, yellow, and key (black). Though the printing process varies by print house, press operator, press manufacturer, and press run, ink is typically applied in the order of the abbreviation (CMYK). The "K" in CMYK stands for key, since in four-color printing, cyan, magenta, and yellow printing plates are carefully keyed or aligned with the key of the black plate. (Some sources suggest that the "K" in CMYK comes from the last letter in "black" and was chosen because B already means blue.) The CMYK model works by partially or entirely masking colors on a lighter, usually white, background. The ink reduces the light that would otherwise be reflected. Such a model is called subtractive because inks "subtract" brightness from white.

In additive color models such as RGB, white is the "additive" combination of all primary colored lights, while black is the absence of light. In the CMYK model, it is the opposite: white is the natural color of the paper or other background, while black results from a full combination of colored inks. To save money and to represent deeper black tones, printers create unsaturated and dark colors by using black ink instead of the combination of cyan, magenta, and yellow.

Over the years, there has been an argument regarding the existence of three primary pigments for printers that work as well as the primary inks, dyes, and chemicals used in painting and dyeing (red, yellow, and blue). Cyan, magenta, and yellow, are aligned with the physiology of human color perception, and in printing, their combinations can yield all colors. The ability to manifest these three colors in pigments does not currently exist. Perhaps chemists will eventually succeed in formulating a true red, a true yellow, and a true blue pigment primary for the printing industry.

Color photographers also use cyan, magenta, and yellow to develop color using dyes and gelatin emulsions. Colored film contains three layers of emulsion that respond to blue, red, and green light. Each layer forms one of the three dyes that are the subtractive primaries—cyan, magenta, and yellow.

### Red, Yellow, and Blue (RYB)

RYB predates much of modern scientific color theory, which has demonstrated that cyan, magenta, and yellow are the best three colorants to combine to achieve the widest range of high-chroma colors. RYB is the one used by painters, printmakers, and illustrators working with acrylics, oils, pastels, and inks. For artists working with these traditional techniques, the primaries are considered red, yellow, and blue. Since most two-dimensional foundation courses' color projects are done using paint, ink, or colored paper, the remainder of this chapter will focus on subtractive color and consider the primaries to be red, yellow, and blue.

## Color Wheel

Color wheels depict the relationships of the basic colors and are the most common way to organize them. Even with the simplest color wheel models, controversies have arisen over which few hues are the basic ones from which all other hues can be mixed. There are at least five different possibilities that seem to be true, depending on the situation. This book presents the circular arrangement of the color wheel based on a subtractive system of artist-pigmented colors using red, yellow, and blue as primaries. This triadic primary system has evolved over many centuries. The triadic primary color system used in this book for discussion is the Munsell color wheel.

### History of the Color Wheel

Our modern understanding of light and color begins with Sir Isaac Newton (1642–1726) and a series of experiments that he published in 1672. He was the first to understand the rainbow, and refracted white light with a prism, resolving it into its component colors: red, orange, yellow, green, blue, and violet. To prove that the prism was not coloring the light, he refracted the light back together. Through his experimenting with light, he eventually added the color indigo, a red-violet color not found in the spectrum. This color acted as a transition between violet and red and enabled him to insightfully twist what was up to that point a straight-lined spectrum. When he joined the two ends, he created the first known color wheel and placed complementary colors opposite one another.

Around 1731, J. C. Le Blon discovered the primary characteristics of the pigments of red, yellow, and blue, and their ability to create orange, green, and violet. To this day, his discovery remains the basis for much of pigment color theory.

Around 1766, an English engraver named Morris Harris published the first color chart printed in full hue. This chart appears in the book *The Natural System of COLOR's*. It discusses the primary colors (red, yellow, blue), the mediate colors (orange, green, purple), and compound colors (tertiaries). This is the point most color theorists consider the true beginning of color theory.

From the 1800s on, there is a flurry of activity in the study of color. The men who took up the study of color came from varied backgrounds of scientists, philosophers, artists, and even poets. Johann Wolfgang von Goethe arranged his colors in both circles and triangles, Philipp Otto Runge used both the triangle and a solid color sphere, and Charles Blanc arranged his colors in a six-pointed star. The amount of information available is overwhelming and often contradicting and conflicting. The history presented up to this point is simply to illustrate how long it took man to develop a logical system for studying color and to show how varied the methods can be.

## Atlas of the Munsell Color System

Theoretically, because color has three attributes or dimensions, each individual color can be placed as a single point in an abstract, three-dimensional space—called a color space—with similar colors situated close to each other. Such space can then be sliced into a series of two-dimensional color diagrams or maps, which would make up a color atlas.

The best-known subtractive atlas, the Atlas of the Munsell color system, was developed by the American painter Albert Henry Munsell (1858–1918) and published in 1915. It formulated a color system to show the relationships between different color tints and shades based on the three properties of color: hue, value, and intensity.

The Munsell model is visually described as a tree, where the "trunk" has 10 brightness steps of value, from black at the bottom to white at the top. The hues encircle the tree trunk and their intensity changes from neutral at the trunk to pure hue at the extremities. In the Munsell system, the five basic hues are red, yellow, green, blue, and indigo (purple).

In 1943, the US Bureau of Standards adopted the Munsell system for naming colors. The most important part of the Munsell color system is the color notation, which describes a color in terms of a letter and numerical formula. The notation found on the inner circle of the color wheel indicates a hue. The numbers on the central trunk indicate the value of the colors. The numbers on the vanes that radiate from the trunk show the intensity, or chroma. These value and intensity relationships are expressed by fractions, with the number beneath indicating the intensity (chroma).

**Color System**

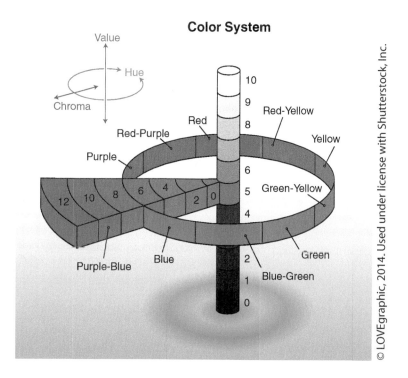

© LOVEgraphic, 2014. Used under license with Shutterstock, Inc.

This perspective diagram graphically illustrates the three dimensions of color used by the Munsell color chart for color measurement and notation. This illustration is intended merely to help visualize the three scales in as graphic a form as possible by a printed diagram. The first dimension is hue, measured on the band or equator shown in perspective as encircling the central pole. This is divided into 10 equidistant hues arranged in the order of the spectrum: red, yellow-red, yellow, green-yellow, green, blue-green, blue, indigo-blue, indigo, red-indigo.

In the second dimension of his color wheel, Munsell defines value. It is measured on the central pole, and divided into regular steps from dark to light. This dimension shows how light or dark a color may be. Step 0 on the value pole in the center is black (the darkest gray possible) and step 10 is the lightest white (complete absence of gray). In mixing colors, an absolute black and white are not practically attainable.

The third dimension on this Munsell color wheel is chroma, measured on the paths (shown in perspective) running from the neutral pole out, This dimension measures the weakness or strength of a color. The chroma scale of blue is shown here at middle value, from neutral out to the maximum strength, The chroma paths of the other hues are indicated in outline only. Each of these paths may be drawn from any other step on the value scale.

## Color Wheel Categories

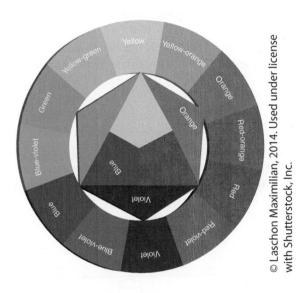

Although the primary, secondary, and intermediate colors differ between additive and subtractive color systems, a color wheel is used to both organize and represent the relationships of basic colors. For discussion, the color spectrum will be broken down into 12 hues, which are divided into three categories, primary, secondary, and tertiary colors arranged as a triadic color system.

# Primary Hues

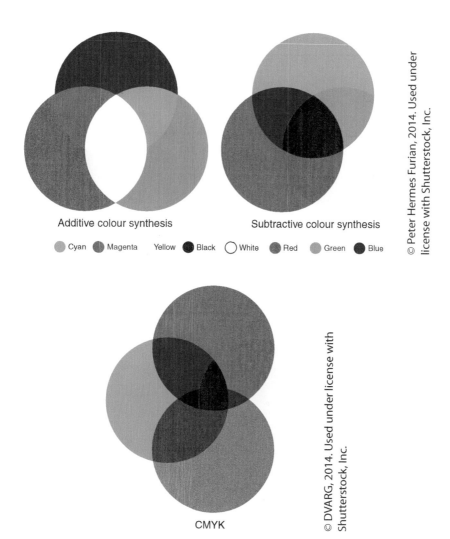

Additive colour synthesis        Subtractive colour synthesis

⬤ Cyan   ⬤ Magenta   ⬤ Yellow   ⬤ Black   ⬤ White   ⬤ Red   ⬤ Green   ⬤ Blue

CMYK

A primary color is one of three colors, from which all other colors can theoretically be mixed. By definition, they are the colors that cannot be created by mixing other colors. The primaries of pigments are traditionally considered red, yellow, and blue. For printing, primaries are considered cyan, magenta, yellow, and key black. Primaries in light are red, blue, and green. The most commonly used additive color primaries are the secondary colors of the most commonly used subtractive color primaries, and vice versa.

When you have completed the following three assignments, you will have created an entire color wheel by mixing the subtractive primary colors together.

# ASSIGNMENT 3.26

In your sketchbook, create a value scale by mixing red and yellow. Make sure each individual step is defined and the transition equitably distributed across all 10 steps as you progress from yellow to red. Each individual value scale is to be comprised of 1" x 1 1/2" painted rectangles glued down in a linear arrangement. It is more economical to gradually mix red into the yellow pigment.

# ASSIGNMENT 3.27

In your sketchbook, create a value scale by mixing yellow to blue. Make sure each individual step is defined and the transition equitably distributed across all 10 steps as you progress from yellow to blue. Each individual value scale is to be comprised of 1" x 1 1/2" painted rectangles glued down in a linear arrangement. It is most economical to add blue to the yellow pigment.

# ASSIGNMENT 3.28

In your sketchbook, create a value scale by mixing blue to red. Make sure each individual step is defined and the transition equitably distributed across all 10 steps as you progress from blue to red. Each individual value scale is to be comprised of 1" x 1 1/2" painted rectangles glued down in a linear arrangement.

## Secondary Hues

A secondary color is the mixture of two primary colors. With pigments, these are orange (red + yellow), green (yellow + blue), and indigo (red + blue).With light, the secondary colors are yellow (red + green), magenta (red + blue), and cyan (green + blue). With printing, the secondary colors are blue (cyan + magenta), red (magenta + yellow), and green (yellow + cyan). Like the primaries, these three hues are equidistant from one another on the color wheel. They are called secondary because each is theoretically born of primary parents.

## Intermediate Hues

An intermediate hue is any mixture of a primary with a secondary neighboring color. Because a change of proportions in the amount of primary or secondary color used will change the resultant hue, many subtle changes are possible. Intermediate colors are often mistakenly called tertiary colors but this is technically incorrect. Tertiary colors are made from a mixture of all three primaries in differing amounts or two secondary colors. Tertiary hues do not appear on the color wheel. They are found in the inner circle of a color wheel and are characterized by a loss of intensity and a neutralization of hue. A complete neutralization occurs with an equal mixture of complementary colors.

Intermediate colors are produced from mixing primaries red, yellow and blue (RYB) pigments' with secondary colors orange, indigo and green. These produce amber (yellow-orange), vermilion (red-orange), magenta (red-indigo), violet (blue-indigo), viridian (blue-green), and chartreuse (yellow-green). The colors produced from this mixing are considered third-generation hues because combining a primary with a secondary hue forms these colors. These six intermediate colors all have hyphenated names that indicate the two source colors. The name of the primary color is listed first.

RYB pigments' tertiary colors made from mixing two secondary colors are russet (orange-purple), olive (purple-green), and citron (green-orange).

Red, green blue (RGB) and cyan, magenta, yellow, black (CMYK) primary and secondary colors produce tertiary colors: azure (cyan-blue), violet (blue-magenta), rose (magenta-red), orange (red-yellow), chartreuse (yellow-green), and spring green (green-cyan). Secondary mixed with another secondary are russet (orange-purple), slate (purple-green), citron (green-orange), plum (russet-slate), sage, (slate-citron), and buff (citron-russet).

## Neutrals

© aoo3771, 2014. Used under license with Shutterstock, Inc.

Not all pigments contain a perceivable hue. As mentioned in the last chapter on value, when no color quality is found in a neutral black, white, or gray, they are referred to as achromatic. Since there is no color, what distinguishes one achromatic neutral from another is the quantity of light they reflect. Because achromatic neutrals do not have color, they are not represented on the color wheel.

A neutral white reflects all of the color wavelengths equally and can be thought of as the presence of all color. Black absorbs all color wavelengths equally and reflects none of them. Black is considered to be the absence of color. Absolute black rarely exists; therefore most black pigments contain some trace of reflected color. It is impossible to get an absolute black in an additive color system; the closest you will get is a dark gray.

Any gray is an impure white because it is created by only partial reflection of all the color waves. The closer to black a gray gets, the less reflective the surface. It is considered a light gray if it reflects a lot of light and considered a darker gray if the light reflected is low. When discussing neutrals, an artist is mainly concerned with the quantity of light reflected. When discussing colors, an artist's focus is more on the quality of light reflected.

A neutral can also refer to a color that has been mixed with its complement. This type of neutral would not exist on the outer ring of the Munsell color wheel, but would be located toward the center of the color wheel. A composition using neutrals will be harmonious because strong hue contrasts are not possible.

## Triadic Color System

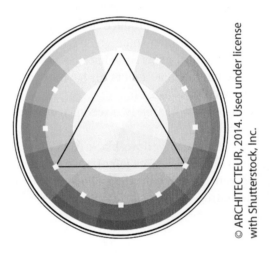

© ARCHITECTEUR, 2014. Used under license with Shutterstock, Inc.

A triadic color system is a theory of organizing colors as a color wheel. It places three primary colors equally spaced apart on a wheel. These colors form an equilateral triangle, called a primary triad. The diagram above depicts a primary color triad for pigments: red, yellow, and blue. The three secondary colors are placed between the primaries from which they are mixed; evenly spaced, they create a secondary triad and would be represented by an equilateral triangle connecting orange, green, and purple. Intermediate colors placed between each primary and secondary color create equally spaced units known as intermediate triads. They would be represented by a triangle connecting red-orange, blue-purple, and green-yellow, as well as an equilateral triangle connecting yellow-orange, red-purple, and blue-green. Cumulatively the primary, secondary and intermediate color triangles comprise a 12 -color wheel.

The closer colors are to one another on the color wheel, the better their hues relate to each other. The further apart colors are on the color wheel, the larger the difference between them. Hues directly across from each other have the least in common and generate the greatest contrast. They are known as complementary colors. In a triadic system, the complement of a hue is theoretically the combination of the other two points (colors) of the triangle equally mixed. For example, the complement of red is green and the triadic triangle theoretically represented would include blue and yellow (the two colors from which green is derived). This demonstrates that a color and its complement will represent an entire primary triadic color system. Another example of finding a color's complement in a triadic color system would be to start with yellow. The other two colors in this triadic color system would be blue and red, because a triadic color system is represented by the colors found in an equal-sided triangle spaced on a color wheel. The complement of yellow is purple, a mixture of red and blue. In short, to find the complement of a secondary hue, first identify which primary colors are mixed to form the secondary color; the remaining member of the triad (the only primary not used) will be the mixed color's complement.

## Color Schemes

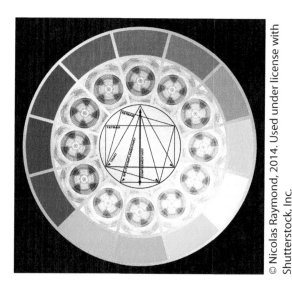

A composition ought to evoke a sensation of pleasure or discomfort through a unified organization of the art elements. Color is one of the strongest art elements used by artists as a means of expression. A combination and arrangement of color on the picture plane develops and conveys content or meaning. A single color can create character, mood, and emotional responses in a viewer, but when compared to the artistic expression that can be achieved in a unified relationship with other colors, it can feel very restrictive and limiting to an artist. The successful use of color depends on understanding some basic color relationships or schemes.

An artist's command of color schemes is based on information gathered formally through instruction, assignments, critiques, and reading art psychology studies. Informally, artists learn from classmates and viewer responses. Art foundation textbooks and courses like this one are where a basic understanding of making art is developed. To develop a basic understanding of color, a young artist needs to study, experiment, and create with color. In this regard, color is consistent with how the other art elements have been introduced in this textbook. Building upon small successes with the art elements individually will develop artists' ability to express themselves through a unified composition.

Color is a perfect tool to unify a design that might not be apparent in the initial pattern of shapes. In general, the more complicated and busy the pattern of shapes is, the more an artist needs to restrict her use of color. If the shapes are larger and simple, an artist may need to explore exciting color schemes to breathe life into the design. Color theory has been developed to help artists and designers make good choices. The art of using one of these color schemes is to vary the ratios of the color, rather than distributing them in equal measures.

An artist has many color schemes to explore with compositions. An experienced artist will be able to tell a story to the viewer from across the room. A color scheme needs to get and maintain the viewer's attention and convey her intent. In the hands of an experienced artist, each color scheme has a unique ability to express ideas differently. This section will introduce ten ways to organize color schemes: monochromatic, complementary, split complementary, double complementary, analogous, triads, tetrads, cool, warm and discordant color schemes. The following color schemes are all based on Munsell's color wheel.

## Monochromatic

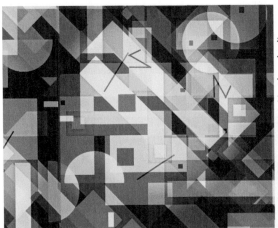

A monochromatic color scheme is the simplest type of scheme. It consists of only one hue, but can explore the color's complete range of brightness and variations in saturation. Tints and shades derived from mixing white and black with a principle color are included in this color scheme.

The monochromatic color scheme is easy to manage, because it always looks balanced and visually appealing. Monochromatic colors, by default, go well together. A monochromatic color scheme heightens a viewer's awareness of, and places an emphasis on, shape and texture. This scheme looks clean and elegant. When created in cool blue or green hues, it produces a soothing effect as well. The visual effect is, of course, extremely harmonious and generally quiet, restful, and (depending on the range of values) subtle. A high level of unity exists with this type of color scheme because it shares a common hue. Unfortunately, this shared hue can be an impending disadvantage as well. Even with thousands of variations of tints and shades of one color, this scheme is potentially the most uninteresting due to a lack of variety for the viewer.

## Complementary

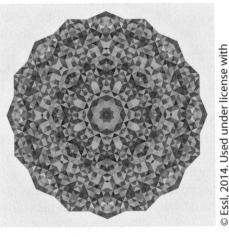

A complementary scheme, as the term implies, joins and is built around two hues that are opposite one another on the color wheel. This scheme is intrinsically high in contrast and intensity, to the point of creating vibrating colors when juxtaposed. This occurs because when viewing a color, only that color's wavelength is being reflected and the wavelengths not being reflected equal the color's complement. Therefore an agitation occurs when two complements are placed nearby, because of their great contrast. Each color increases the apparent intensity of the other color, and when used in equal amounts, they are difficult to look at for any length of time due to simultaneous contrast. Reducing the amount of one of the colors or introducing changes in the intensity and value level of one or both can overcome simultaneous contrast.

An artist's color palette noticeably increases when he uses a complementary instead of a monochromatic color scheme. Visually, mixing complementary colors lowers the intensity and produces an amazing range of browns. When paired in a composition, complementary colors are ideal partners. Each increases the distinctive strengths of the other. In compositions, these hues produce a lively, exciting pattern especially if the colors are used at their full intensity. Red and green, which are closest in value, create extreme agitation when placed side by side. Violet (a dark value) and yellow (a light value) when mixed together represent and produce the widest value range. Because their value range is further apart, they do not agitate each other as much. By mixing two complements plus black and white, we can create a range of colors that begins to suggest the power of a full spectrum.

Complements are pairs of colors that are opposite each other on the color wheel. The true meaning of the word complement is "to make complete" or "to perfect something." Any two complements contain the complete trio of primaries. For example, yellow and its complement, violet (made up of red and blue), complete the primary trio—yellow, red, and blue. Thus complementary colors complete and perfect the fundamental role of the primary colors as the essence of all colors.

The tertiary colors and their complements follow the same rule. Each pair of tertiary complements is made up of the three primaries. For example, yellow-green is the complement of red-violet. If you think it through, you will see that yellow-green contains yellow and green (made from blue + yellow). Its complement red-violet contains red and violet (made from red + blue). These tertiary complements, therefore, also contain the complete primaries—yellow, red, and blue—again perfecting the primary triad. The most successful tertiary color themes incorporate a dominant color and use its complementary color for accents. Because of the high contrast factor, this color scheme must be managed well so that it does not appear too jarring. Often tints, tones, and shades of the complementary color are used to soften the look.

Another unique feature that artists have historically explored is a visual phenomenon called afterimage. If you stare at an intense color for a minute or so and then look at a white background, the complementary color will appear.

## Split Complementary

© Lynda Lehmann, 2014. Used under license with Shutterstock, Inc.

A split complementary color scheme is composed of the principle color and the two colors on either side of its complement. Split complementary color schemes tend to have slightly less contrast and more subtle variations than a complementary color scheme. This is understandable since the artist has the potential to create more variety because a split complementary color scheme involves mixing three related hues rather than just two, as previously described under complementary schemes.

The split complementary provides high contrast without the strong tension of the true complementary scheme.

## Double Complementary

© Victoria Kalinina, 2014. Used under license with Shutterstock, Inc.

A double complementary color scheme is based on a combination of four colors. It can also be thought of as two overlapping true complements. The double complements are spaced on either side of an "imaginary" true complement. For example, if true complements were orange and blue, then their double complements would be yellow-orange and blue-violet plus green and red. The double complementary color scheme is the richest of all of the schemes because it uses four colors. This scheme can be hard to harmonize particularly if all four colors are used in equal amounts, so you should choose one color to be dominant or use tints, shades, or tones of the other colors selected. A double complementary scheme uses two sets of complementary colors and if they come from equidistant places on the color wheel, this is termed a quadrad.

## Analogous

© GalinaL, 2014. Used under license with Shutterstock, Inc.

An analogous color scheme combines several colors that sit next to each other on the color wheel. This scheme is based on a pie-shaped slice of at least three, and up to five, hues located next to each other on the color wheel, usually with one hue in common. Analogous schemes are the most harmonious because three of the four neighboring hues used always contain at least one common color that dominates the group. Physically, analogous colors are inherently harmonious because they reflect light waves that are similar. This is also the reason that analogous hues blend so well visually. They are most harmonious when the middle color in the scheme selected is a primary color: for example, blue-green, blue, and blue-purple. As with the previously described color schemes, the hues in an analogous color scheme may vary in value. As with monochromatic harmony, a high degree of unity is ensured, but the wider range of hues offers greater variety and can increase interest.

Analogous schemes are natural and thus more comfortable. Because of this, they can give the appearance of seasonal effects such as yellow to green in the spring or yellow to red, gold, and brown in the fall. Such effects lead to the use of analogous schemes to give a sense of coolness or warmth where desired.

## Triads

© Victoria Kalinina, 2014. Used under license with Shutterstock, Inc.

Another type of complementary color scheme, in which three colors are used, is called a triad. A triadic color scheme is any set of three hues that are equidistant on the color wheel, forming the vertices of an equilateral triangle. Examples of triadic schemes are violet, orange, and green; and red-purple, yellow-orange, and blue-green.

A primary triad uses the primary colors and is the most common and easily identified triadic scheme. It provides the liveliest set of colors and creates striking contrasts.

A secondary triad is softer even though the interval between the hues is the same, because any two secondary colors will be related through their commonly shared primary. For example, a triad that contains points of orange and green will share yellow.

There are two intermediate triads on a twelve color wheel. As we move further away from the purity of the primaries, the contrast among the colors in these two triads is softer. This occurs because intermediate colors incorporate more colors from the color wheel. As a result, there are even shorter intervals between colors, producing less contrast.

The triad is one of the most useful formulas for harmony and it is often used in decorating to form pleasing color schemes. Because triads use colors that are unrelated, they can be difficult to work with. To use triadic harmony successfully, the colors should be carefully balanced. An artist should let one color dominate and use the two others for accents. If the color looks too harsh, tints and shades of a triad can be used to soften this effect of unrelated colors. This scheme is often used when variety and a strong impact are essential.

## Tetrads

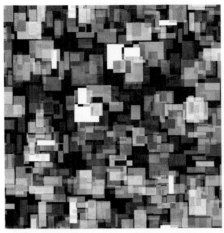

© Tanor, 2014. Used under license with Shutterstock, Inc.

A tetrad color scheme is based on a square. This system is formed when four colors are used in the organization. These hues are equally spaced around the color wheel and contain a primary, its complement, and a complementary pair of intermediates. An artist should try to avoid using all four colors in equal amounts. The increased variety will make the composition even more interesting. A tetrad color scheme works best if you let one of the colors be dominant. You should also pay attention to the balance between warm and cool colors in your design.

## Cool Colors

© Africa Studio, 2014. Used under license with Shutterstock, Inc.

Cool colors are considered the hues found on the color wheel between red-violet and green. Cool colors tend to be psychologically soothing. When viewed, they can physically lower the blood circulation and thereby decrease body temperature. They also are called cool colors because their hues remind us of cool things like water, plants, and ice.

Cool colors have a tendency to feel like they are receding or backing away from you because of their darker value. Often designers will paint the walls of small rooms with cool colors to make them appear more spacious.

## Warm Colors

© danielo, 2014. Used under license with Shutterstock, Inc.

Warm colors include hues on the color wheel between red and yellow-green. These colors tend to remind us of warmth and excitement like the sun or fire. Warm colors tend to be more exiting and can actually make people feel warmer because they can slightly increase blood circulation and body temperature.

Warm colors have the opposite effect on space than cooler colors do. Warm colors will tend to optically advance in space. Colors like deep red can make large spaces appear to be more intimate. A soft yellow can make a dreary room feel more cheerful and sunnier.

## Color Discord

© hakne1, 2014. Used under license with Shutterstock, Inc.

The artist's goal is to create a sense of unity within the composition and a congruency between his idea and the arrangement of the art elements. If an artist's idea pertains to an uncomfortable topic, then using an analogous color scheme would not be the right color system. On the other hand, a discordant color scheme is in synch with his idea. This develops a positive relationship between his idea and materials. Yes, it is possible to use discord and develop a sense of unity. When skillfully used, color disharmony can be as effective as color harmony.

Color discord is the opposite of color harmony and conveys an immediate negative impression. As in life, discord is unwelcomed, but at the same time, it provides a stimulus or element of excitement. In art, a discordant color scheme acts similarly. If it were not for discord, we would not know harmony. Mild discord results in exciting, eye-catching color combinations. A discordant color in a composition may contribute visual surprise and better express certain themes or ideas. Colors widely separated on the color wheel, but not complementary, are generally seen as discordant combinations. A discordant color combination involves colors that have no affinity with each other. They tend to have a combative rather than harmonious relationship.

Artists need to be attentive to value when developing discordant color schemes. The discord between two colors is greater when they are similar in value. This is because the lack of value contrast focuses the viewer on the actual disharmony of the hues. The higher the value contrast between the hues, the less disturbing they will be visually to the viewer. This happens because the viewer is focusing primarily on the contrast between the values and secondly on their hue.

## Understanding the Color Wheel and Hue

At this point in the chapter, you should have a working knowledge of the vocabulary of color and understand how to construct a color wheel. Next you will learn how to identify the values and intensities of colors. And finally you will learn how to create harmonious compositions.

### Identifying a Color

When investigating color, the first question you should ask yourself is: What is the basic source of color for a hue? The answer to that question is one of the 12 hues on the color wheel. Without considering the lightness or darkness of this color or its brightness or dullness, which of the basic 12 color wheel hues is the starting point? Your answer to this question will determine your starting point on the color wheel.

The second question you should ask yourself is: How light or dark is this color relative to a 10-step value scale from white to black? Compare the color to your value chart and determine a value between 1 and 10. Research shows that seven or so value steps are about the maximum a human can retain in visual memory.

The third step is naming the intensity of the color. Intensity, as defined earlier, is the brightness or dullness of a color. The next question to ask yourself is: How bright or dull is this color relative to an intensity scale? Intensity will range from the brightest color possible, one of the pure color wheel hues, to the dullest color possible, where the color is so dull you cannot discern any hue at all in it.

After determining the color's intensity, proceed to mix the hue with white to brighten it or its complement to dull it. Adding a color's complement is the best way to lower its intensity without changing its value.

### Complications Seeing Color

There are three factors that complicate "seeing" or identifying a color. Color consistency states that we see colors we expect to see and negate the local color of an object. For example, we all would agree that grass is green. In reality, the local color of grass can range from green to blue to gray depending on the time of day. The other two reasons complicating our ability to accurately see color are even more difficult to control. Two adjacent colors will each influence how the viewer will perceive the other color, as explained by simultaneous contrast. Finally, the unexpected effects of light on color will distort our understanding of color.

# ASSIGNMENT 3.29

Obtain a color swatch from your instructor and paste it into your sketchbook. With this assignment, you will be trying to mix your paints and match its hue, value, and intensity. Keep a procedural diary of working notes as you physically mix your paints. After you have achieved a match, describe in writing your problem-solving thought process. Place both in your sketchbook.

# Local, Optical, Arbitrary Color Use

The discovery of new colors during the 16th century led to a shift in painting from shape-based compositions to designs that focused on and celebrated color. There are three basic ways in which color can be used in painting: objective, optical, and arbitrary.

## Objective

Objective color is when an artist reproduces the colors as seen in white daylight. These are the colors that we would mentally associate with objects based on our interactions. With an objective color scheme, the artist's choice is primarily determined by the subject matter and not as determined by variations in light. This color use is also sometimes termed local color.

## Optical

Optical colors are the hues you will see once your eyes override your mind's labeling of an object's color. Various lighting conditions as well as the time of day play an important part in determining optical colors. Artists rely on optical color to reproduce the visual image. They accurately document the colors they see, but in this case under illuminations other than natural white daylight. The interrelated relationship between color and light is exemplified with this painting approach.

## Arbitrary

The third kind of color approach clearly reflects artists' approach to painting in the 20th century. Arbitrary color ignores the natural colors of objects. Instead, the color created is based on heightened visual effect, compositional needs, desired emotional responses, or is purely contrived by the artist's imagination.

# Color in Composition

Color's role in a composition is complex. It is used to spatially develop and unify the picture plane, create a mood, express personal emotions and feeling, attract and direct a viewer, balance a composition, or simply help identify the appearance of an object.

The effect of color on a composition's balance and a shape's visual weight are equally dramatic. The color balance determines the overall unity of a composition. First of all, this is determined by the placement and relationship of the colors to one another. A unified design would establish a harmonious relationship with just enough variety to keep our attention. Color more than any other art element has the capacity to attract a viewer's attention. Color also has an inherent visual weight that can be used to balance any composition. An artist must concern himself with balancing the color composition and ensuring that the color scheme visually supports his idea or intent. Balancing a composition through color involves a lot of manipulation and a strong understanding of color.

Artists use color, as they do the other art elements, to give highly personalized meaning to the subject of their work. There are no exact rules for arriving at pleasing effects in color relationships, but there are guiding principles from which every artist develops her own language of color.

With color, the simplest way to relate elements of a design is to select a scheme that has a common color and place these colors throughout a composition. This is one of the strengths of a monochromatic color scheme. Varying the value or intensity of the color will introduce variety while maintaining a strong sense of harmony. An option to using a monochromatic color scheme would be to utilize an analogous color scheme in which there was a common hue.

While developing a composition, artists need to remember that too much of one thing is not good. In this case, the drawback of color is that quite quickly it can become over harmonized. Developing compositions that have a more dominant color, by adding contrast, or by introducing a variety of colors are all ways to introduce variety as color to a composition. The biggest obstacle you will find when working with contrasting color schemes is to unify the contrasts without destroying their general strength and intensity of expression.

Another way to unify a design with color is to introduce a similar amount of color repeatedly throughout a composition. If the shapes are similar in size and color, they will help unify the overall composition. While focusing on distribution and proportions within a design, an artist will be directing viewers to key points he wishes them to experience. Color can be used to increase the compositional importance of a visual element. Using a contrasting color, value, size, or intensity are just a few ways to use color to develop a focal point.

Color schemes are used to develop pleasing color relationships or structures. From the start, artists must decide the color scheme that most appropriately expresses their idea.

Color can shift visual balance, create a focal point, influence our emotions, and expand communication. Our perception of colors changes according to their surroundings. Even in the same light, a color will appear different depending on the colors that are adjacent to it. The colors on the color wheel are shown at their inherent values. This inherent or normal value is the pure color unmixed and undiluted. Thinning a color with water or paint thinner will alter a color's value. The more transparent a color, the lighter value it will appear to have when placed on a white background. Mixing a color with a different hue will alter the value of a color. Value, like color, is a variable and depends on the surrounding hues for its visual sensation. Colors are also changed by their context. The quantity and repetition of color within a composition are also critical factors in color interactions.

## Tonality

Often an artist will use color to unify discordant elements in a composition. When a single color dominates a composition, despite the presence of other colors, or its importance permeates a composition's entire color structure, this type color unity is called tonality.

When colors are chosen from one part of the color wheel, they will share one hue in common. Monochromatic color schemes are the obvious example of tonality being used to unify a composition. Because of the single common and dominant hue of analogous schemes, they also can be described as having uniform tonality.

## Depth of Field

Colors have an innate advancing or receding quality because of slight muscular reactions in our eyes as we focus on different colors. Intense, warm colors (red, orange, yellow) seem to expand and come forward; cool colors (blue, green) contract and appear to recede. As objects recede, any brilliance of color becomes more neutral, finally seeming to be gray-blue. This physiological fact enables artists to create the illusion of an object's volume, flatten an area, or develop a sense of depth on the picture plane.

Hues and values themselves may be used as clues of spatial organization. The greater the contrast in value and/or hue between two areas, the greater the distance between them will appear. The stronger the contrast between figure and ground, the further apart they seem to be in space. Colors appear to exist more and more on the same plane as they approach a common value and similar hue.

Most artists use atmospheric perspective to align the composition's picture plane. A naturally occurring phenomenon is that receding objects visually appear to become gray-blue in color and less brilliant in intensity. An object's value, intensity, and color contrasts are also more pronounced in the foreground and subtler in the distance. These visual effects are so commonplace that we are inclined to interpret cool colors as receding even in abstract art.

Many abstract artists have used the relationship of balance and movement in space to give content to a composition even though no actual objects are represented. Line, value, shape, and texture are greatly aided by the ability of color to create space and meaning. Through our color choices, we can cause various areas in a composition to expand or contract visually. This sense of pushing and pulling in an artwork can be a major source of energy in a nonobjective composition.

# Psychology of Color

Color can be organized by more than its physical properties. It may also be organized by its ability to create mood, symbolize ideas, and express personal emotions. By itself, color can express a mood or feeling, but when combined with a shape, especially a recognizable one, its psychological power is intensified. A color's hue, value, and intensity are equally important to the emotional impact. In a composition, strong contrasting values placed beside each other suggest vitality and robustness, whereas closely related values with low intensities create feelings of reserve and calmness.

Color permeates our daily lives and we are continually exposed to the application of color's emotive power. It is present in our language, our environments, and our clothes. As a result of our daily interaction with color, it becomes emotionally charged. Nowhere is the psychology of color more apparent than in retail sales. Retailers know that light and bright colors make us feel joyful and uplifted, that warm colors are stimulating, while cool colors are calming. Generally, cool dark or somber colors are depressing.

In art, the power of color to symbolize ideas becomes a tool. It enriches the metaphor and makes the work stronger in content and meaning. Colors are never emotionally neutral. They contribute to the overall emotion of the design, pictorial depth, and can create tension or power through contrast. An artist will use yellows, oranges, and reds to give us an instinctive feeling of warmth and evoke warm, happy, cheerful reactions. Compositions with cooler blues and greens are automatically associated with quieter, introverted feelings and can express melancholy or depression.

We cannot escape the emotional effects of color because color appeals directly to our senses and is a psychological and physiological function of sight itself.

Johann von Goethe's research marks the beginning of color psychology. His studies provide a general exposition of how color is perceived in a variety of circumstances. Because of his studies, we have come to understand the distinction between the optical spectrum that Sir Isaac Newton discovered and the phenomenon of human color perception. Goethe linked, for example, red with a festive mood, suggestive of imagination. He chose the primaries red, yellow, and blue for their emotional content and he grouped the different subsections of his color triangle by elements of emotion—lucid, serious, mighty, serene, melancholic—as well as by mixing level. The effect of colors may be purely psychological, but their influence is very real.

Colors of the spectrum may be just wavelengths of light, but the colors we see and their uses are subjective and come with cultural and psychological associations. Colors have an effect on both minds and bodies. Throughout one's life, the significance of color changes. As children, we tend to be attracted more by color than by shape, but as we mature, shape becomes more important. We may become more form dominant as we grow older, but creative people often remain color dominant all of their lives.

Color is an amazing vehicle for expressing emotions and feelings not only on a personal level but on a cultural level as well. Different eras and diverse cultures invent different color symbols. Although a specific meaning of a color may vary widely from culture to culture, every culture assigns symbolic meaning to specific colors.

In contemporary society, symbolic color designations are associated with political, religious, and commercial messages. This is extremely evident in advertising and marketing. As you become more aware of visual language, you will become attentive to how advertisers manipulate it (and you). The good news is that by studying the art elements and design principles, you will become more conscious and able to diffuse this influence.

The relationship between color and society is in a constant state of fluctuation. It varies between cultures, by the decade, and daily with an individual's mood. As artists, we reflect and produce culture. Understanding the emotional expression of color within a cultural context is extremely important in the development and understanding of our visual language. The potential for color to attract and direct a viewer's attention as well as give meaning and organization to a composition is unsurpassed.

# ASSIGNMENT 3.30

Using color, create and label designs in your sketchbook that reflect the following emotions or states of mind: (1) anxiety, (2) hope, (3) fear, (4) submission, and (5) contemplation.

## Optical Mixing

Realizing that pigments will never reproduce the luminous and brilliant quality of light, artists tried various techniques to overcome this limitation. One attempt is called visual color mixing or optical mixture. With this technique, artists place pure colors side by side in small areas and the viewer's eyes optically mix them together. This new color only exists in the viewer's mind rather than being physically mixed by the artist on a canvas.

This approach to producing art is often associated with the post-impressionist era of the late 19th century and can be observed in the artworks of Seurat and van Gogh. Pointillism juxtaposes pure colors to achieved color sensations. In a way, these artists anticipated the truly additive color mixing that occurs on a laptop screen.

Visual mixing is the reason four-color printing works. In this printing process, different sized dots of cyan, magenta, yellow, and black reproduce all the colors in an image, or on a computer screen, where luminous dots of red, green, and blue more successfully capture the colors of reality.

This is the excitement of color. Depending on how you place colors together, even a limited number can produce the illusion of three-dimensional forms and define a depth of field.

## Simultaneous Contrast

Michel Eugène Chevreul developed the theory of simultaneous contrast. It states that whenever two colors come into contact, their similarities will decrease and their dissimilarities will be enhanced. In short, this simultaneous contrast intensifies the difference between colors. The phenomenon is most evident in complementary colors, but also occurs, albeit to a lesser degree, when two colors are related. Blue is at its most vibrant and will seem to vibrate when it is next to orange, as will green when it is placed next to red.

There are three principles of simultaneous contrast. The first is the contrast of light against a dark background. This principle states that a white or lighter background will darken a color and a dark color background will lighten it.

The second principle involves complementary reactions. Simply put, when surrounded by the complement of a color, the color will be heightened. Complementary hues, when placed alongside of one another contrast so intensely that an optical illusion occurs in our visual perception apparatus. Our eyes are pulled back and forth along the shared edge and the colors seem to vibrate. Often viewers claim that a third color appears along this edge. At the point your head becomes confused with what is happening; the artwork becomes a living thing with myriad shapes appearing and disappearing.

The third principle states that the characteristics of intensity, value, and hue can trigger simultaneous contrast. A blued-gray will look brighter when placed against a gray background and tends to make the gray take on an orange cast. When warmer colored hues are placed against cooler hues, the basic characteristics of each of them are heightened. The warmer hue will appear warmer and the cool cooler. As a rule, a hue tends to bring out its complement in a neighboring color. If a neutralized gray made by mixing two complementary colors (for example, blue and orange) is placed next to one of the complements being mixed (blue), the gray will take on a hue that is the complement of the color (orange).

Complementary colors produce another phenomenon called afterimage. Afterimage explains why if you stare at a color for a minute or so and look at a white background, the original color's complement appears. Afterimage is the result of retinal fatigue. Prolonged exposure to a single hue will cause the receptors for that color to fatigue while the receptors for the color's complement will still be perceived.

## Summary

Color is amazing and a powerful art element. With a thorough understanding of color and value, and enough technical proficiency, an artist is able to suggest a three-dimensional form and locate it in space. Color can increase the power of a given shape, shift compositional weight, and create a focal point. It can enhance the illusion of space, suggest volume, and heighten emotion.

When understood and technically applied, color is one of the most expressive elements of art and design. It stimulates your senses or can help you relax. With color, you can create a mood. A well-chosen color scheme can transform and literally add value to your home. This power of color comes from its ability to produce physiological as well as psychological reactions in people.

# SECTION 4

## Space

# Space

The creation of depth on a two-dimensional plane is an illusion. The images rendered on paper, canvas, or boards are flat, but through the manipulation of the art elements, the suggestion of space can be achieved. Through the illusion of space, an artist invites viewers to enter an imaginary world.

Some authors regard space as an element in its own right. In this textbook, space will be regarded as the result of the art elements as structured through the principles of organization. However space is classified, the concept of space is unquestionably of crucial importance and a basic knowledge of its implications and use is essential for every artist.

In this textbook, space will also serve as a means to review the art elements and principles of organization, as well as concepts discussed in the previous chapters.

## Spatial Perception

Vision is the result of our eyes sending an image that our mind interprets. Over the years, our visual experiences shape and form our spatial awareness. There are two types of vision, stereoscopic and kinesthetic. Stereoscopic vision refers to our ability to merge two separate images into a single image. This visual process enables us to see three-dimensionally, judge distance, and perceive a depth of field. In art, we experience kinesthetic vision when our mind unconsciously attempts to organize and understand the separate information our eyes have gathered as they move across an artwork.

An art element's spatial position begins to be defined as soon as a contrasting mark is applied to a background. In order to develop an overall sense of unity, an artist needs to develop a consistency between his idea, the art elements, and the spatial indicators.

## Spatial Indicators

To develop the illusion of space, an artist can use spatial indicators such as size, position, overlapping, transparency, interpenetration, position, fractional representation, sharp and diminishing details, and more formal spatial systems such as linear perspective. In addition, many spatial experiences can be achieved by manipulating the art elements: position, number, direction, value, texture, size, and color.

## Types of Space

In two-dimensional compositions, an artist can develop two types of spatial illusions: shallow and deep space. Shallow space is confined to the flatness of the picture plane and lacks any real or suggested illusion of depth. In shallow space, a shape of uniform color and value will be perceived as flat and as only existing on the picture plane. The second type of space, deep space, is any type of spatial illusion other than shallow. With deep space, the picture plane only exists as a starting point where the suggestion of space begins. Size, position, overlapping images, sharp and diminishing details, converging parallels and perspective are all used to suggest deep space.

## Developing the Illusion of Space

For an artist, the easiest and quickest way to develop space is through varying the size of the art elements. In general, our personal experience has proven to us that the larger an object, the closer it is to us, and the smaller an object, the further away it visually appears. The image below exemplifies overlapping, transparency, interpenetration, and vertical placement as means to develop the illusion of space.

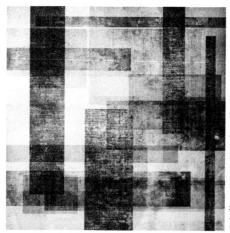

## Overlapping

Experience has also conditioned us to believe that if two objects are placed one in front of the other, the object closer to us will block our ability to see the portion of the second that is located behind it. Overlapping presides over the other spatial signs except when transparency is being applied to the composition.

## Transparency

In an attempt to acknowledge the continued existence of the unseen portion of a three-dimensional object blocked by the placement of another object, the concept of transparency was developed. Transparency is similar to overlapping, except the overlapping planes of an object are represented in their entirety. Transparency does not give us a clear spatial pattern and can change as we look at it. This purposeful ambiguity is called equivocal space and often results in visual confusion for the viewer. An artist often uses it to develop the illusion of motion.

## Interpenetration

Interpenetration is similar to both overlapping and transparency in that the relationship between at least two objects defines the spatial plane of a composition. It describes the visual illusion of when one plane or shape appears to pass through another and reemerge once again. Our brain believes this illusion because of visual linking concepts.

## Vertical Placement

The vertical placement of an object on the picture plane may be used to suggest the spatial depth perceived by a viewer. The higher an object on the picture plane, the further back in space the mind will perceive it to be located. Both an artist and observer automatically assume that a horizontal line will be interpreted as the horizon line or eye level. The horizon reference is an integral part of vertical location. An object placed above the horizon line is considered to be off in the distance. Objects below the horizon line or along the bottom of the picture plane are seen as the closest visual points. Vertical location is based on visual facts and memories that are congruent with our physical experiences. Looking out onto the horizon, the ground at our feet is the closest point of reference. As we raise our eyes and look out to the distance, objects gradually move farther away, until our eyes reach eye level or what in linear perspective is referred to as the horizon line. When vertical location is congruent with size, together they can provide a very effective illusion of space.

## Fractional Representation

Historically, fractional representation has been used by various cultures, most notably Egyptian and was once again explored by Cézanne in the 19th century to suggest spatial depth. Fractional representation combines several spatial aspects of the same subject into one image. Doing this entails the representing of multiple perspectives in one design.

## Types of Linear Perspective

Credited to Filippo Brunelleschi, linear perspective is another technique that historically has been utilized to depict space. Linear perspective is based on the visual phenomenon that as parallel lines recede, they appear to converge and to meet on an imaginary line called the horizon or eye level and involves the application of spatial indicators as size, position, and converging parallels. It was the dominant device for spatial representation in Western art for several hundred years. Linear perspective systems automatically organize and unify the lines and planes of an object and represent it realistically.

There are three major systems of linear perspective. Each is based on viewing the subject matter with one eye closed from three different positions—above, below, or at eye level—while maintaining a fixed point of reference.

## One-Point Perspective

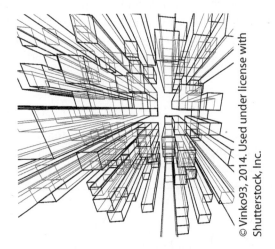

© Vinko93, 2014. Used under license with Shutterstock, Inc.

With one-point perspective, the artist views a flat surface or facing plane directly, or head on. With this system, the artist first establishes the horizon line, which represents the eye level. If the object is below the artist's eye, then the horizon line is placed low on the page. If it is above the artist's eye level, then the horizon line is placed higher up on the picture plane. Next the artist identifies where the vanishing point is located on the horizon line. All of the lines recede to the one common vanishing point located on the horizon line.

The vanishing point is located directly in front of the artist on the horizon line. As a rule, vertical lines stay vertical and horizontal lines stay horizontal. These lines remain constant and are measurable. With one-point perspective, the artist begins the drawing with the shape's portion closest to the viewer. Extending guidelines from the shape determines and represents the depth of space the shape occupies and defines the object's side-walls. One-point perspective works best with a subject that has a flat frontal view.

# Two-Point Perspective

© Vladis Chern, 2014. Used under license with Shutterstock, Inc.

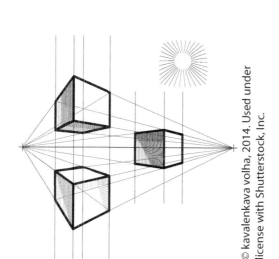

© kavalenkava volha, 2014. Used under license with Shutterstock, Inc.

Two-point perspective involves the edge of two intersecting planes. This edge is the closest part to the viewer. With two-point perspective, all of the planes will appear to recede and converge at two vanishing points located on the horizon line: a right vanishing point (RVP) and a left vanishing point (LVP). With a two-point perspective, the artist places himself in front of a corner of a room or building so that no planes are parallel to the picture plane and the sidewalls recede back to different points located on the horizon line.

As in a one-point perspective, the artist begins by establishing the horizon line. Its placement in the picture plane once again corresponds to the height of the artist's viewing position. Next, LVPs and RVPs are located on the horizon line at the extreme left and right ends. They represent the farthest extreme points our eyes can see. The vertical lines representing the corner edge of the object indicate the height of where the volumes come together. Only verticals can be measured and they never converge in two-point perspective drawings. From the top and bottom of the center, vertical diagonal lines are extended back to the vanishing points on either side of the central vertical. These diagonal lines establish the sides, top, and/or bottom planes of the geometric solid. These planes appear to get smaller as they converge toward the vanishing points. In a two-point perspective drawing, all lines, except for those that are vertical, recede to one of the vanishing points along the horizon line.

# Three-Point Perspective

© danielo, 2014. Used under license with Shutterstock, Inc.

A three-point perspective is used to represent an exaggerated point of view of objects positioned very much above or below the horizon line. In three-point perspective, the top and bottom edges converge to distant points. These are sometimes referred to as worm's-eye or bird's-eye points of view.

Once again, the artist begins by locating the horizon line that best represents the location of the viewer's eyes, and fixing the LVP and the RVP at the appropriate location on the horizon line. The next step gives a three-point perspective its name. The artist locates a third point called the vertical vanishing point (VVP), along a vertical axis, running perpendicular off of the horizon line. The location of the VVP is determined by the viewer's position along the horizon line. The VVP also controls the distortion of the object—the further away from the horizon line the third point is located, the less exaggerated the image will be.

Like a two-point perspective drawing, the artist starts by drawing a vertical line to represent the object's corner that is nearest to him. Lines are extended back to the vanishing points after the artist decides the length of the corner vertical closest to him. These diagonals become and define the sides of the object. To create a three-point perspective, the artist finally needs to project the top or bottom plane of the shape. This placement depends on where the shape is located in reference to the horizon line. If the shape is above the horizon line, then the artist will extend vertical lines from the vertical edge to the VVP located above the horizon line. If the shape is positioned below the horizon line then the vertical lines of the vertical edge are extended to the VVP positioned below the horizon line.

## Summary of Linear Perspective

Linear perspective approximates what our eyes see, but its limitations have caused it to be less popular in the 20th century than in preceding periods. Many artists object to the restraints perspective entails. Linear perspective involves the application of such spatial indicators as size, position, and converging parallels. The artist's compositional freedom consists of the placement of the horizon, vanishing points, and the first line. From that point, the drawing becomes a mechanical drawing. Linear perspective is merely another tool for artists to employ when appropriate or ignore when they wish. Understanding how to apply an atmospheric perspective to linear perspective helps create a more convincing illusion of spatial depth.

# ASSIGNMENT 4.1

Photocopy images of one-, two-, and three-point perspectives and paste them into your sketchbook. Tape a sheet of tracing paper over top of each image and on it identify the horizon line, vanishing points, receding planes, and on the three-point perspective identify the VVP.

# Atmospheric Perspective

© Dave Allen Photography, 2014. Used under license with Shutterstock, Inc.

The notion of diminishing details is the basis of an aerial or atmospheric perspective drawing. In this type of drawing, the artist is attentive to the effect the atmosphere has on the appearance of an object as it is viewed from a distance. As the distance between an object and a viewer increases, the contrast between the object and its background decreases, and the contrast between any markings or details within the object decreases. With an atmospheric perspective, the colors of the object also become less saturated and shift toward the background color, which is usually blue, but under some conditions may be another color.

With aerial or atmospheric perspective, an artist uses color and value to show depth. In deep space, both the value contrasts of distant objects and a shape's contour become less pronounced than the value contrast or contour of an object depicted in shallow space. Colors behave similarly; as an object moves off into the distance, the object's colors neutralize and take on a bluish character.

Texture is a tougher art element to control. Objects placed in shallow space have physically larger, sharper defined, and higher contrasting surfaces than objects perceived farther off in the distance. As an object moves off into deep space, its texture gets smaller physically; the pattern has less defined or crisp boarders; and the pattern has less contrast.

## Spatial Properties of the Art Elements

In addition to the many spatial techniques explained thus far in this chapter and in the rest of the book, spatial effects can be achieved by manipulating the art elements' position, number, direction, value, texture, size, and color. The rest of this chapter is dedicated to reviewing how a sense of depth or the illusion of space can be developed by manipulating the spatial properties of the art elements.

### Line and Space

A long and thick line appears closer to the viewer than a short and thin line. When lines overlap, they define their different spatial positions, especially when their placement contrasts with one another. In defining space, vertical and horizontal lines appear more static than diagonal lines, which are able to activate space by moving from the picture plane back into deep space.

### Shape and Space

When used spatially on the picture plane, a shape may refer to planes, solids, or volumes. A plane exists two-dimensionally when it is placed parallel to the picture plane, but three-dimensionally when placed on its edge.

## Value and Space

Where the light source is located will determine the value placement within a composition. If the light source is positioned in front of a composition, the areas closest to the light or foreground will be represented by a lighter value. Objects in the middle and background of the composition will be represented with progressively darker values as they move back from the picture plane. Finally, a darker value will recede and define deep space, as long as it is in low contrast to the shapes surrounding it.

As with atmospheric perspective, the details of the composition follow similar guidelines. Objects in the foreground are seen with clarity and great contrast, while distant objects are less defined and gray. Therefore neutral grays, when juxtaposed with blacks or whites, generally take a distant position.

## Texture and Space

Generally speaking, sharp, clear, large, and bold textures advance, while fuzzy, dull, and minuscule textures with low contrast recede. The physical size of the texture is relevant to the spatial illusion it develops in the composition. A physically larger texture will advance in comparison to smaller textures of equal contrast. Within the texture itself, if a texture is highly defined and has a high degree of contrast, it will pull forward on the picture plane and a texture consisting of the opposite characteristics will recede into deep space.

## Color and Space

Analogous colors, because they are closely related, create limited spatial movement, whereas high contrasting colors enlarge the space and provide varied accents or focal points of interest. Both exploit the limitless dimension of space.

When an artist can combine an understanding of linear and atmospheric perspective with the knowledge of how to manipulate the art elements, a convincing representational illusion of space can be achieved.

# Recent Concepts of Space

Our search to understand and represent the world has brought about a new awareness of space. Technology has enabled artists to view the world from many new perspectives and as a result they are no longer content with the limited historical techniques to represent space.

In our society, motion is evident everywhere. From the personal expression of YouTube videos and video games to public entertainment and advertisements, moving images constantly bombard us. Contemporary artists are aware of and are exploring the power of movement and its ability to create space. Advancements in technology are enabling artists to present ideas never conceived of before. As a result, a new dimension has been added to our spatial conception, the fourth dimension. The fourth dimension combines space, time, and motion.

The exploration of space in terms of the fourth-dimension space–time continuum is in its infancy, but all indications suggest that it will give artists an opportunity to contribute to and reflect on the ever-changing aspects of individuals and society.

# GLOSSARY

**Abstract**
A term used to represent the presentation of an object that has been simplified and reduced to its basic essentials. Only the fundamental aspects of a form or concept are presented. All extra details are removed.

**Abstract Art**
One of the major forms of nonrepresentational and semi-representational art. It started with Cubism, during the second decade of the 20th century and reached a peak about the middle of the century.

**Abstract Form**
A form that has been reduced, distilled, or transformed down to resemble its original source.

**Abstraction**
The reduction of an image or object to the essential form or concept. The simplification or rearrangement of the appearance of natural objects or nonrepresentational objects to fulfill the artists' ideas or needs for visual organization in a composition. Abstraction is present in varying degrees, in all works of art, from full representation, to complete nonobjectivity.

**Abstract Shape**
A derived shape that has been so transformed that it barely resembles the original source.

**Abstract Expressionism**
A 1940s American style of painting characterized by a nonrepresentational style that stressed psychological or emotional meaning.

**Abstract Texture**
An edited texture used purely for decorative effect with no intent to fool the viewer. Abstract texture is derived from an actual surface that has been rearranged and simplified into stylized patterns to meet the artistic needs of a composition.

**Academic**
Art that is practiced and taught in Art Academies. It conforms to established traditions and standards as well as stresses standards, set procedures, and rules.

**Accent**
Any art elements, in a composition, that attract more attention than the others that surround or are close to them. Usually created through color, tones, size, or any other means to attract attention. (See Dominance.)

**Accent Color**
A color used to attract attention to a specific part of a design.

## Achromatic (Value)

The difference of light and dark value. It is black, white, and all of the grays in between, but has no hue or intensity.

## Achromatic Grays

Grays made from mixing only black and white together with no other color.

## Actual Lines

Physically present, real, or existing lines in a design.

## Actual Shape

A shape with distinctly defined boarders or a "positive" area. (The opposite of an implied shape).

## Actual Texture

A surface that can be seen visually as well as physically experienced through touch.

## Additive Color

Color produced by superimposing light rays' three physical primaries: red, blue, and green.

## Aerial Perspective

A technique used to create the illusion of deep space, in which distant objects have less detail and contrast than nearer objects, are lighter in value, and reflect a bluish color shift. (Also called atmospheric perspective.)

## Aesthetic or Aesthetics

The study of aesthetics combines philosophy, psychology, and sociology of art and no longer focuses on what is beautiful, but instead attempts to discover the origins of sensitivity to art forms and the relationship of art to other aspects of culture such as science, industry, religion, and so on.

## Afterimage

The appearance of the complementary color produced after staring at an intense color and then quickly refocusing on a white surface.

## Alignment

A unifying arrangement of shapes so that their edges are perceived to create a continuous visual line or to line up.

## Allover Pattern

The repetition of designed units into a readily recognizable systematic organization that covers the entire surface and lacks an obvious focal point. The entire two-dimensional surface is emphasized. Also called crystallographic balance.

## Alternating Rhythm

A rhythm created by regularly and interchangeably repeating two or more art elements or motifs in an anticipated basis.

## Amorphous Shape

A formless shape that lacks clearly defined and obvious edges or dimensions.

## Amplified Perspective

A dramatic effect created when distorted objects projecting toward the viewer are drawn in perspective.

## Analogous Colors

Colors closely related in hue(s) and usually situated near or adjacent to each other on the color wheel.

## Analogous Color Scheme

A color scheme based on three or more hues, positioned next to each other on the color wheel, that most often share one common hue.

## Anomaly
A visual relief or break from the perceived design norm.

## Approximate Symmetry
A composition that contains very similar imagery on either side of a perceived visual axis but contains enough variation to maintain a viewer's attention. (See Near Symmetry.)

## Arbitrary Color
Unnatural colors that are produced by the artist's imagination, selected to convey an emotional response, or used purely for a visual effect.

## Art
Communicating an idea through a chosen medium.

## Assemblage (art style)
Often associated with Rauschenberg and Kienholz, this style of art brings together rather bulky individual three-dimensional objects that are displayed in their original position rather than being limited to a wall.

## Asymmetrical Balance
An artwork balanced through the uneven physical distribution of parts throughout, rather than having a visible or implied axis; without symmetry. (See also Informal Balance.)

## Atectonic
A term used to describe a type of sculpture characterized as open, with extended appendages, as opposed to massive (or tectonic).

## Atmospheric (Aerial) Perspective
The illusion of deep space created, by an artist, on a two-dimensional plane, by lightening values, softening details and textures, reducing value contrasts, and neutralizing colors.

## Attached Shadow
A shadow that directly reflects and is defined by the shape of a form from which it is cast.

## Axis
An imaginary visual line around which a form or composition is visually perceived to be balanced.

## Background
In a two-dimensional design, the area behind the subject, positive, or figure.

## Balance
One of the principles of organization; a sense of equilibrium achieved through implied weight, attention, attraction, distribution and/or emphasis of the art elements, distributed on either side of an axis, in order to accomplish unity.

## Bauhaus
Staatliches Bauhaus, commonly known simply as Bauhaus, was a school in Germany that combined crafts and the fine arts, and was famous for the approach to design that it publicized and taught. It operated from 1919 to 1933.

## Bauhaus School
The Bauhaus school was founded by Walter Gropius in Weimar. It was founded with the idea of creating a "total" work of art in which all arts, including architecture would eventually be brought together. The Bauhaus style became one of the most influential currents in Modernist architecture and modern design. The Bauhaus had a profound influence upon subsequent developments in art, architecture, graphic design, interior design, industrial design, and typography.

### Bezold Effect

An optical illusion, named after a German professor of meteorology, Wilhelm von Bezold (1837–1907), who discovered that a color may appear different depending on its relation to adjacent colors. In design, it is when the total effect of the perceived hues used is altered by the change of one dominant hue.

### Biaxial Symmetry

A guaranteed type of balance in which top and bottom (vertical) as well as left and right (horizontal) axes of symmetry are the same. Top and bottom can be the same as the left and right, or they can be different.

### Biomorphic Shape

Irregular shapes characterized by curves derived from organic or natural forms found in live organisms.

### Bird's-Eye View

A drawing in which the viewer is placed high on the picture plane looking down and most objects are presented below the viewer's eye level.

### Bridge Passage

Where two adjacent parallel planes are gradated in opposite directions, from dark to light and light to dark, there will be an area where differences of value dissolve.

### Brightness

A color's relative lightness or darkness.

### Calligraphy

Rhythmical, elegant, decorative, and flowing lines used in artworks that are suggestive and transcend the literal contents of writing.

### Canon

A measuring module based on mathematical proportions used to arrive at an ideal representation.

### Cast Shadow

The dark area created on a surface by an object blocking the light source.

### Characteristic Texture

An inherent texture or the familiar texture that is commonly associated with a material or object.

### Chiaroscuro

The technical representation that blends light and shade gradually to create the illusion of three-dimensional objects in space. Chiaroscuro comes from the Italian words, chiaro for clear or light, and oscuro for obscure or dark. It is often used to refer to the dramatic and theatrical compositional styles of Caravaggio and Rembrandt.

### Chroma

Refers to the intensity or purity of a hue. It is the complete lack of white, black, or gray in a hue. (See Saturation.)

### Chromatic

Pertaining to the presence of color.

### Chromatic (Value)

The perceived lightness or darkness demonstrated by a given color.

### Chromatic Gray

A gray created by mixing various hues, rather than the introduction of black and white.

### Classical

Derived from the ancient art of Greece, in the fourth and fifth centuries BC, it refers to an art form characterized by a controlled, clear, and intellectual approach.

## Classicism

The application or adherence to Greek cultural ideals of beauty, and purity of form, style, and techniques, by later cultures, such as Roman and Renaissance civilizations, and the art of the Neoclassical movement in the early 19th century.

## Closed Composition

A composition in which the elements are contained within the edges of the canvas or the picture frame. (See Open Composition.)

## Closed-Value Composition

A composition in which the edges of a shape define, limit, and contain the values.

## Closure

A concept borrowed from Gestalt psychology that states an individual will view incomplete information as complete and as a unified whole. With closure, the artist takes advantage of the observer's desire to perceive incomplete forms as complete. The artist provides minimum visual clues and the observer brings them to final recognition.

## CMYK

A graphic design color system in which successive printings of cyan, magenta, yellow, and black visually mix to produce the necessary colors. Also known as four-color printing.

## Collage

A two-dimensional art technique in which real materials are combined with painted or drawn images. From the French verb caller, meaning to glue or stick.

## Color

A visual response to the wavelengths of sunlight broken down into hues. Possessing the physical properties of hue, saturation, and intensity (brightness).

## Color Constancy or Constancy Effect

A feature of the human color perception system which ensures that the perceived color of objects remains relatively constant under varying illumination conditions. For example, a green apple looks green to us at mid-day, when the main illumination is white sunlight, and also at sunset, when the main illumination is red. The psychological concept to explain the discrepancy between actual color and the color we assume to be correct.

## Color Discord

A visually unharmonious color scheme created by using colors widely separated on the color wheel.

## Color Harmony

Visually harmonious color relationships based on groupings within the color wheel. (See Analogous and Complementary Colors.)

## Color Interaction

The way colors relate and influence each other within a composition.

## Color Key

A dominating color, in an image, that heightens its psychological and compositional impact.

## Color Space

The abstract three-dimensional space a color occupies based on its three attributes or dimensions—hue, value, and intensity—with similar colors placed close to each other.

## Color Symbolism

The use of color to represent or simulate human character traits or express an artistic concept.

## Color Tetrad

Four colors equally spaced on the color wheel, consisting of a primary, its complement, and a complementary pair of intermediates. Color tetrads may also be any organization of colors on the wheel that form a rectangle and that may also include a double split complement. (See also Complementary Colors, Split Complementary Color Schemes.)

## Color Triad

An equilateral triangle formed by three equally spaced colors on the color wheel.

## Color Wheel

An arrangement of colors based on the sequence of hues in the visible spectrum, arranged as the spokes of a wheel.

## Color Theory

The study of color interactions and their effects in art and science.

## Combining

Collecting items to isolate them from the rest of the composition. In Gestalt theory, combining is one of the four main types of proximity: nearness, touching, overlapping, and combining.

## Complementary Colors

Represented by two colors directly opposite one another on the color wheel. The mixture of two primaries will produce the complement of the third primary color. When placed next to each other, complementary colors become accentuated. When they are mixed, they neutralize each other.

## Complementary Color Scheme

A color scheme characterized by high contrast and at times, intensely vibrating colors; consisting of two hues positioned opposite one another on the color wheel.

## Composition

An arrangement of the art elements on a two-dimensional plane, as governed by the principles of organization, that achieves visual unity.

## Concept

A comprehensive idea or scheme intended to bring the art elements into a visual relationship.

## Conceptual Art

An approach to making art that appeared in the 1960s. The main focus was on "idea," which defined the materials and final form of an artwork.

## Constructivism

A movement founded in Russia 1919 and associated with Vladimir Tatlin's Tower. It focused on the rejection of art for art's sake and emphasized art's social purposes. Combined machine aesthetics with mechanical objects.

## Content

Content refers to the significance, expression, and essential meaning we understand—or the subjective, psychological, or emotional properties we feel—in a work of art.

## Contextual Integration

The process of ensuring that the presentation or arrangement of the art elements reinforces or supports the artist's idea.

## Continuation

A process in which either real or implied lines or aligned art elements enable a viewer to move through a composition easily.

## Continuity

When a designer unifies the presentation of information so that two or more pages have a visual relationship to one another. Used often in publications or website designs.

## Contour Line

A line used to define the outermost exterior or edge of an object. (Often referred to as an "outline.")

## Contrast

An arrangement of opposite elements in a piece to create visual interest, excitement, or drama used to direct a viewer's attention. The colors white and black provide the greatest degree of contrast. Complementary colors also highly contrast with one another. Other examples of contrast are light vs. dark, rough vs. smooth textures, large vs. small shapes, and so on.

## Contrasting Colors

The use of colors that appear to be different in hue, value, intensity, or temperature (warm or cool.)

## Cool Colors

The hues yellow-green to violet are considered to have cool subjective temperatures. These are colors we associate with water, ice, rigidity, and so on. (See also Warm Colors.)

## Core Shadow

The darkest part of an object; attached to the object and not directly illuminated by the light source.

## Craftsmanship

A technical aptitude or skill level one possesses. The quality of workmanship determined in handling tools and materials.

## Cross-Contour

A line that undulates across a shape as it defines the surface within the outmost edge of a shape.

## Cross-Hatching

Lines made at right angles to the original hatch lines. They are used to develop value and volume, and to suggest form. (See also Hatching.)

## Crystallographic Balance

A form of balance that places equal emphasis "allover."A two-dimensional composition with crystallographic balance has no focal point and the viewer's eye is guided nowhere and everywhere, all at the same time. (Also known as allover pattern.)

## Curvilinear

Shapes that emphasize curved lines. Often inspired by organic shapes found in nature.

## Deep Space

The illusion of "as far as the eye can see." Also referred to as infinite space.

## Definition

The discernable difference between a shape and the background or other shapes in a composition. Sharply defined shapes advance and blurred shapes tend to recede on the picture plane. Definition can also be the degree of resolution or focus within a composition.

## Depth of Field (DOF)

The distance between the nearest and farthest objects on a picture plane or in a composition.

## Descriptive (art)

Art that adheres to as much of a likeness to the actual object as possible.

**Descriptive Shape**
A shape derived from and accurately depicted from a specific subject matter.

**Design**
A structured plan by which an artist arranges the visual elements of a composition. Design may be considered synonymous with the terms form or composition.

**Direction**
The actual or implied movement of an element in a design.

**Dissonance**
Discord most often created in a composition using disharmonious colors, shapes, textures, or sounds. A dissonant composition lacks harmony.

**Distribution**
The visual arrangement of the art elements to create a composition on the picture plane.

**Dominance**
A principle of organization, where certain art elements are emphasized or are given prominence over others in the composition or design.

**Double Complementary Color Scheme**
Two sets of complementary colors that are equidistant on the color wheel. Also referred to as a quadrad.

**Drawing**
An artwork where the predominant feature of the composition is line.

**Dynamic Range**
A value range of pigments usually from white or the lightest to black or the darkest in a composition.

**Economy**
The distillation of an image to its barest essentials for clarity of presentation; one of the principles of organization.

**Elements**
The basic components an artist uses to produce the visual language of art: line, shape, value, texture, and color.

**Elements of Design**
The basic building blocks from which an artist makes art.

**Emphasis**
Manipulating the art elements to draw a viewer's attention to a specific area of a composition.

**Equilibrium**
When opposing compositional elements, while being placed about an axis, are brought into visual balance.

**Equivocal Space**
An optical illusion in which the viewer vacillates between the figure and ground or the positive and negative shapes in a composition. The ambiguous space causes visual confusion and engages the viewer with the artwork.

**Explicit Line**
A line or edge that stands out from the background and clearly delineates a form.

**Expression**
The thought, emotion, or meaning as presented through visual objects. (Synonymous with content.)

## Expressionism
A form of art in which more emphasis is placed on what is felt rather than perceived or reasoned.

## Eye Level or Eye Line
Eye level, or the horizon line, is determined by the physical position of the artist in a linear perspective drawing. It is the line on which all vanishing points are positioned.

## Fibonacci Series
By definition, the first two numbers in the Fibonacci sequence are 0 and 1, and each subsequent number is the sum of the previous two. Used with cabalistic reduction in Islamic art. (See also Golden Ratio.)

## Figure
The object being depicted or the positive shape.(See also Ground or Figure/Ground Reversal.)

## Figure/Ground Reversal
When the positive and negative shapes in a composition alternatively fight for and command the viewer's attention. (See also Equivocal Space.)

## Flat Color
An area of even color that contains no value variations. Often called match or spot color in graphic design.

## Focal Point
In a composition, the area(s) that an artist decides to emphasize to attract the viewer's attention. (See also Accents.)

## Font
A complete set in one size of all the letters of the alphabet, along with associated ligatures, numerals, punctuation marks, and other signs and symbols.

## Forced Perspective
The suggestion of deep space created by using unnatural or smaller physical properties of objects in a composition.

## Foreground
The part of the two-dimensional picture plane closest to the viewer when an illusion of depth has been created.

## Foreshortening
A visual effect in which the parts of an object further away from us are drawn smaller than if they were viewed straight on in order to create the illusion of three-dimensional space as perceived the by a viewer.

## Form
The actual three-dimensional object or the suggestion of three-dimensionality depicted on a two-dimensional plane. Form may also refer to the organization of the visual elements (according to the principles of organization) to produce a unified artwork.

## Format
The outermost edge or exterior boundary of a design.

## Formal
The execution of a composition based on strict design rules.

## Formal Balance
The representation of exact or similar elements on either side of the central axis. (Also referred to as symmetrical balance or mirrored image.)

### Four-Dimensional Space
A design format that gives a sense of intervals of time or motion.

### Fractional Representation
A device used by various cultures (notably the Egyptians) in which several spatial aspects of the same subject, such as the front view of an eye on a side view of the head, are combined in the same image.

### Genre
A genus, style, category, or class of an art having common content, form, technique, or the like.

### Geometric Form
A form that is derived from or suggestive of mathematical formula.

### Geometric Shape
Simple shapes that can be defined by mathematical formulas or produced using the implements found in geometry sets such as triangles, rectangles, and circles.

### Gestalt
A German word for "form."

### Gestalt Psychology
Theory developed by Czech-born psychologist Max Wertheimer. The Gestalt psychologists promoted the theory that explains psychological phenomena by their relationships to total forms, or Gestalten, rather than their parts. The four main Gestalt properties are proximity, similarity, continuation, and closure. Based on the concept that an organized whole is greater than the sum of its parts.

### Gesture Drawing
A drawing in which the exact presentation of the form is secondary to capturing the dynamics of a scene or pose. It imitates the natural movement of the viewer's eye within and around a form.

### Golden Ratio or Mean
A traditional proportional system discovered by the ancient Greeks for developing visual harmony based on a mathematical ratio found in natural forms. It states that the whole is divided into two sections such that the smaller part is to the larger as the larger is to the whole. The ratio is 0.618:1 or 1:1.618 or roughly 8:13. Having "perfect" harmonious proportions.

### Graduated Tint
A continuous value change in which no distinction or discernable breaks are observable.

### Gradation
Any gradual transition from one color, shape, or volume to another. In drawing, three-dimensional forms can be created through shading or the presentation of gradations of gray.

### Graphic Art
A two-dimensional artwork created through the use of the art elements. It also refers to printing techniques used in newspapers, books, magazines, and so on.

### Gravity
In design, the physical experience that suggests the placement of objects high on the picture plane will naturally fall to the bottom.

### Grid
A network of horizontally and vertically intersecting lines that provides a structural framework for a designer to use while placing objects on the picture plane; helps unify a composition.

## Grisaille
A monochromatic version of chiaroscuro in shades of gray or a neutral color, which imitates the appearance of low relief sculptures.

## Ground
The unoccupied space located within the picture frame, usually referred to as the background. Traditionally, the figure is a positive shape; the ground a negative shape. It is as important a contributing factor to a composition as the figure. (See also Figure.)

## Group
A collection of images perceived to be related because of a common subject matter, placement in a composition, and so on.

## Grouping
The visual organization of similar items together. Gathering of elements based on a common location, orientation, shape, color, and so on.

## Harmony
One of the principles of organization used to unify a composition. Often considered the adhesive used to combine art elements into a visually pleasing and consistent composition. Achieved most often through the repetition of similar characteristics.

## Hatching
Repeated strokes of an art tool to produce clustered thin lines (usually parallel) to create value. In "cross-hatching," similar lines pass over the hatched lines in a different direction, usually resulting in darker values.

## Hieratic Scaling
The practice in early art and some nonwestern cultures in which the increased size or proportion of figures denoted status or importance.

## High-Key Color
Any color that has a value level of middle gray or lighter.

## High-Key Value
A value that has a level of middle gray or lighter.

## Highlight
The portion of an object that receives the greatest amount of direct light. The area of highest value of a modeled form. Also a bright distinct mark or area on the surface of a shiny form that accentuates its glossiness.

## Horizon
The farthest point we can see; the boundary between the sky and the ground. Also, the line on the picture plane on which vanishing points are located.

## HSB
The preferred terms for the three attributes of color: hue, saturation, and brightness (Intensity). (See also HSL.)

## HSL
In Photoshop, the three attributes of color are known as hue, saturation, and lightness. (See also HSB.)

## Hue
Designates the common name of a color and indicates its position in the spectrum or on the color wheel. Hue is determined by the specific wavelength of the color in a ray of light.

**Human Scale**
Art in which the size of an object relates to the proportions of the human body.

**Hyperrealism**
See Photorealism.

**Idea**
Something, such as a thought or conception, that potentially or actually exists in the mind as a product of mental activity. The plan, scheme, or method set forth by an artist.

**Idealism**
The world depicted as an artist thinks it should be, rather than as in naturalism, in which it is depicted as it is. All flaws and deviations from the norm are corrected.

**Illusion Texture**
See Visual Texture.

**Illusionism**
The imitation of visual reality created on the flat surface of the picture plane by the use of perspective, light-and-dark shading, and so on.

**Illusionary Space**
The suggestion of a three-dimensional object or scene presented or depicted on a two-dimensional surface.

**Illustration**
A type of art that emphasizes telling stories, situations, or anecdotes.

**Imbalance**
Out of equilibrium. When opposing art elements are not visually perceived as being in balance.

**Implied Line**
Imaginary lines, created when our brain joins, completes, continues, or arranges points or short lines that fade, stop, and/or disappear. The missing parts are visually completed or continued by the viewer.

**Implied Shape**
The visual appearance of a shape that does not actually physically exist, but rather is created by a grouping of elements, or psychological connections of dots, lines, areas, or their edges.

**Infinite Space**
The suggestion or illusion of never ending space created within the picture frame. (See also Deep Space.)

**Informal Balance**
The visual balance of dissimilar elements on the picture plane to form a unified composition. Informal balance is more difficult to execute, creates a sense of movement, and generates more curiosity than formal balance. (Also known as asymmetrical balance.)

**Intensity**
Also known as brightness, saturation, strength, or purity of a hue. A high intensity is vivid and a low-intensity hue appears rather dull.

**Intermediate Color**
The result of mixing a primary and a secondary color.

**Interpenetration**
An area of space defined by the illusion of planes, objects, or shapes passing through each other.

## Intuitive Space
The illusion of space suggested by the overlapping, transparency, interpenetration, scale, and fractional representation of shapes on the picture plane.

## Invented Texture
Textures created solely from the artist's imagination, usually resulting in a decorative pattern.

## Isometric Projection (Perspective)
A technical drawing system in which a three-dimensional object is presented two-dimensionally; starting with the nearest vertical edge, the horizontal edges of the object are drawn at a 30-degree angle and all verticals perpendicular from a horizontal base.

## Inverted Symmetry
A form of symmetry in which half of the image is inverted. A style of symmetry often found on playing cards or crossword puzzles.

## Isolation
Denoting or physically separating an art element from others in the composition to create emphasis.

## Kinetic Art
A style of art that incorporates either random or mechanical movement as part of its formal language. Derived from a Greek word (kinesis) that means "motion." (See also Mobile.)

## Kinetic Assemblage
Artwork that is compiled from found objects and incorporates motion or movement as part of its formal presentation.

## Line (actual)
In mathematics, defined as a moving point. In art, a line is a mark made by an instrument or material as it moves across a surface. It is usually made visible because it contrasts with its surroundings. A mathematical line consists of length and direction. In art, a line contains length and direction, but also is considered to contain width, even though this is not its most important feature. Strings, wires, tubes, and so on are examples of three-dimensional lines.

## Line Quality
The weight, direction, and uniformity that define the character of lines.

## Line Weight
The variations of thickness in a line.

## Linear Perspective
A drawing technique used to present three-dimensional ideas on a two-dimensional plane. In linear perspective, objects that are closest to us are represented as being physically larger. It develops the optical phenomenon of diminishing size by treating edges as converging parallel lines that extend back to vanishing points on the horizon line (eye level) and recede from the viewer.

## Local Color (objective)
The familiar color of objects as visually presented under ordinary daylight.

## Local Value
The natural occurrence of lightness or darkness of a surface independent of any effects created by the amount of light projected onto it.

## Lost and Found Edges
When the edges of objects vary from being defined and crisp to disappearing and receding into the background.

**Low-Key Color**
A color possessing middle gray or a darker value level.

**Low-Key Value**
A value possessing middle gray or a darker value level.

**Mass**
In two-dimensional art, a shape that appears to be three-dimensional and stands out from the space surrounding it. Mass can be described as the illusion of bulk and weight achieved by manipulating the art elements or overlapping and merging forms. Three-dimensionally, mass is the actual or apparent physical bulk or solidity of a form or material. Mass is the positive space, and volume is the negative space. (See also Volume.)

**Materials**
See Medium or Media.

**Medium, Media (pl.)**
The material(s) and or tool(s) an artist uses to create the visual elements of a composition.

**Mid-Ground**
The space between the foreground and the background on the picture plane.

**Mid-Tones**
The values located halfway between black and white on the chromatic scale.

**Mixed Media**
Artwork created by combining more than one medium. Often has found objects incorporated into presentation.

**Minimalism**
Abstract artwork reduced down to the barest essential elements required for the form and or idea to be conveyed.

**Mobile**
A type of three-dimensional sculpture popularized by Alexander Calder that involves movement usually activated by the wind.

**Modern Art, Modernism**
A term applied to most avant-garde art made from Impressionism in the late 1880 to the Postmodernism movement of the 1960s. Modern art is mostly nonrepresentational and formally organized.

**Module**
A specifically defined and measured separable component that is interchangeable and assembled with other units of differing size, complexity, or function.

**Moments of Force**
The energy or direction developed in an artwork through the arrangement of art elements in a composition.

**Monochromatic Color Scheme**
Comprised of only one hue including a complete range of value from lightest to darkest.

**Motif**
A repeated object, symbol, shape, color, or pattern, that recurs often enough in a design to become a significant or dominant feature.

**Movement**
The way a viewer's eye travels across the visual pathways developed in a composition. One of the principles of organization.

## Multiple Images

When a single figure or object is presented as multiple superimposed images. This technique is used to represent or suggest physical movement.

## Multiple Perspectives

A drawing or painting technique that presents normally hidden planes of objects to the viewer.

## Multipoint Perspective

A drawing technique to depict space, in which each plane or group of parallel planes has its own set of vanishing points located on the horizon line.

## Munsell System

A tree-like system developed by Albert Henry Munsell for naming colors. The trunk has 10 brightness steps of gray starting with white on top and black on the bottom. Different saturations of color radiate out from the trunk and hues are found along the outer ring. It is related to the HSB system.

## Naturalism, Naturalism (art style)

An art-making approach that mainly focuses on the skillful and descriptive three-dimensional representation of things visually experienced. Pure naturalism contains no artistic interpretation. (The opposite of idealism.)

## Natural Texture

Textures created naturally by forces of nature or natural processes.

## Near Symmetry

A type of compositional balance in which similar imagery is placed on either side of a central axis. The objects are slightly varied to provide visual interest. (Also called Approximate Symmetry.)

## Nearness

The visual phenomenon in which closely placed items are seen as a group. The closer the items, the more likely they will be perceived as a group. One of the four main types of proximity: nearness, touching, overlapping, and combining.

## Negative Area(s) and/or Space

The unoccupied spaces created by the artist's placement of positive objects onto the picture plane; they are as important to the overall success of a composition as the positive elements.

## Neutralized Color

A color that has been grayed or dulled and with its intensity reduced as the result of being mixed with its complementary color or with any achromatic neutral.

## Neutrals

No single color is noticed, only a sense of light and dark or a range from white to black. In an additive color system, it is the inclusion of all color wavelengths to create white or the complete absence of any wavelengths, creating black. In a subtractive color system, it is the alteration of an original hue by adding its complement.

## Nonobjective, Nonrepresentational (art)

Art that is purely imaginative and not associated by the artist or the observer with any previously experienced physical object.

## Nonobjective Shapes

Imaginary shapes that have no reference to shapes found in the physical world. May also be referred to as subjective or nonrepresentational shapes.

## Nonrepresentational
See Nonobjective Shapes

## Objective Art and/or Shapes
Art produced that is based on the physical actuality of an object. This type of art represents objects as appearing natural or real.

## Objective Criticism
Visual assessment of a design based on its perceived strengths and weaknesses.

## Oblique Projection (Perspective)
A technical two-dimensional drawing used to represent a three-dimensional object. The front and backsides of the object are parallel to the horizontal base and the other planes are drawn as parallels coming off the front plane at a 45-degree angle.

## One-Point Perspective
A system developed to suggest spatial illusion on a two-dimensional plane in which parallel lines converge at a single vanishing point usually placed on the horizon line. Best used to represent interiors and landscapes.

## Op Art
Abstract art that has a direct impact on the physiology and psychology of vision or sight; began in the late 1950s.

## Opaque
A surface that is not transparent or translucent and does not allow light to penetrate.

## Open Composition
A composition that implies the partial view of a larger scene due to the arrangement of the art elements being cut off by the picture frame. (See also Closed Composition.)

## Open-Value Composition
Values are not contained within the borders of a shape and are allowed to mix with adjoining areas.

## Optical Color
An object's color that is dependent on the lighting conditions and the time of day. (See Local Color.)

## Orthogonal
Imaginary receding parallel lines at right angles to the field of vision, which join horizontal lines of a building, to the vanishing point. May also be referred to as sight or guidelines.

## Optical Perception
The visual recognition of an object as it truly exists.

## Orientation
The horizontal, vertical, or diagonal position of a composition or the art elements.

## Organic Shape
A shape visually derived from nature or natural forces. (Also known as biomorphic shape.)

## Organic Unity
When the components of an artwork, idea, material, and contextual integration are interdependent, supportive, and relevant to the overall success of an artwork. A work having "organic unity" is not guaranteed to have "greatness" or unusual merit.

## Outline
An actual or suggested line used to describe a shape, its edges, or boundaries.

### Overlapping
A depth cue, in which some shapes are in front of and partially hide or obscure other shapes.

### Paint Quality
The inherent ability of paint to create an interesting texture when applied to a surface.

### Papier Collé
A collage, created from scraps of paper or other two-dimensional found objects glued to the surface of a picture plane. The actual texture of the materials visually enriches and creates a tactile embellishment to areas and functions as a visual richness or decorative pattern similar to an invented texture.

### Pattern
The repetition of an element or motif, in a regularly and anticipated sequence, with some symmetry. Texture involves our sense of touch, but a pattern appeals only to the eye; a texture may be a pattern, but not all patterns have texture design.

### Perspective
A two-dimensional technique used to depict three-dimensional volumes and spatial relationships. There are several types of perspective: atmospheric, linear, and projection systems.

### Photorealism
A painting style intended to look as real as, or more real than, a photograph. (Also called Hyperrealism.)

### Physical Texture
The actual tactile state of a surface.

### Picture Frame
The outermost limit or boundary of the picture plane as defined by the outer edge of a sheet of paper or canvas.

### Picture Plane
The flat surface, usually the surface of the paper or canvas, on which an artist establishes a composition.

### Pigment
A mineral, dye, or synthetic chemical that transfers its color properties to another material by being absorbed, stained, or suspended in paint or ink.

### Pigment Color
The materials in pigments and dyes that absorb, reflect, or retransmit wavelengths of light. The primary colors for pigments are red, yellow, and blue.

### Plane
The position and orientation of a two-dimensional shape or surface that only has height and width.

### Point
In art and design, a term used to describes a dot, a dab, or a blob made by a medium that contrasts with the background on which it is placed.

### Pointillism
A technique for painting in which small, distinct dots of pure color are applied in patterns to suggest an image.

### Positive Areas or Space
The representational or nonrepresentational objects or shapes created through the placement of the art elements or their combination onto the picture plane. (See Negative Area.)

**Positive Shape**
The principle or foreground shape in a design and the dominant shape or figure in a figure-ground relationship.

**Primary Colors**
The foundational hues that cannot be broken down or reduced to component colors from which all other colors can be created.

**Primary Triad**
An equilateral triangle that includes only the three primaries of a 12-step color wheel.

**Principles of Organization**
The rules or guidelines by which visual elements are organized into a unified and expressive arrangement. There are seven principles of organization that guide the employment of the elements in achieving unity: harmony, variety, balance, proportion, dominance, movement, and economy.

**Progressive Rhythm**
Created by regular changes in a repeated element, such as a series of circles that systematically increase or decrease in size.

**Proportion**
The comparative size ratio as measured against the other parts to the whole or against a standard. For example, the Statue of Liberty's hand has a proportional relationship to the size of her head. (See also Scale.)

**Proximity**
The degree of closeness in the placement of elements. In Gestalt theory, the four main types of proximity are nearness, touching, overlapping, and combining.

**Psychic Line**
An imaginary connection created between two points or elements, which directs the viewer's eye in a composition.

**Pure Forms**
Circles, spheres, triangles, cubes, and other forms created without reference to specific subject matter.

**Quadrad**
A double complementary color scheme consisting of two sets of complementaries from equidistant places on a 12-step color wheel.

**Radial Design**
A composition characterized by all of the art elements radiating out from or being balanced around a central point.

**Radial Symmetry**
A form of balance that is created when shapes or volumes are mirrored both vertically and horizontally, with the center of the composition acting as a focal point.

**Realism**
When artists reproduce with a high exactitude what they physically see. (See also Idealism.)

**Rectilinear Shape**
A shape whose exterior consists entirely of straight lines that usually are positioned parallel to the horizontal and vertical. Rectilinear shapes are considered a subset of geometric shapes.

**Reflection**
A type of symmetry represented by a repeating tessellated shape that mirrors itself.

### Repetition
A way to introduce rhythm and dominance of one visual idea into a design by repeating the same visual effect a number of times within the composition until a pattern is produced. An artist uses repetition to develop a harmonious relationship and rhythmic movement.

### Representation(al) Art
When an artist uses the visual art elements so that the viewer is reminded of the actual object. (See also Naturalism and Realism.)

### Representational Shape
A shape strongly derived from the visual observation of a specific subject matter.

### RGB
An abbreviation for the additive primary colors of light: red, green, and blue.

### Rhythm
The repetition of regulated visual units or measured accents to develop a sense of continuance or movement in an artwork.

### Rhythm Relationships
The development of a pulse or beat though the combination of multiple visual art elements or images.

### Rotation
A type of symmetry in which the image of an object is copied and rotated until it intersects or overlaps the original in the sequence.

### Saturation
The strength or purity of a color. The more saturated or purer a hue, the brighter and more intense it appears. A color with no apparent hue is called achromatic-neutral gray, black, or white and is considered to be a desaturated color. (Also known as intensity or chroma.)

### Scale
Relative size as measured against some constant standard or specific unit of measure, mostly relative to human dimensions. (Also see Proportion.)

### Sculpture
The expressive arrangement of three-dimensional materials.

### Secondary Color
The color produced as a result of mixing two primary colors together.

### Sfumato
An Italian term for "smoke" introduced by Leonardo da Vinci to express a transition of value from light to dark produced with such care that the eye cannot detect value changes or distinct tones between values.

### Shade
A hue mixed with black.

### Shadow, Shading
The darker value on the surface of an object that is away from the source of light or being blocked by another object. (See also Cast Shadow or Core Shadow.)

### Shallow Space
A very limited illusion of depth on the picture plane.

## Shape
A two-dimensional enclosed area having width and height, but no perceived depth.

## Silhouette
The shape or total area between or bounded by the contours or edges of an object.

## Similarity
In Gestalt theory, a term for a kind of grouping resulting from the representation of several objects with like characteristics.

## Simulated Texture
A convincing reproduction or translation of an object's texture, created in any medium, by an artist.

## Simultaneity
The practice of superimposing separate views and/or representing different points in time and space to create one integrated image.

## Simultaneous Contrast
The intense contrast created from placing two different colors in direct contact with one another. Simultaneous contrast intensifies the difference between two colors.

## Size
The physical or relative dimensions of an object.

## Space
In three-dimensional art, the area that the art elements occupy. In two-dimensional compositions, the measurable distance or empty area between art elements on the picture plane.

## Spectrum
What one sees after a white light is broken into its component wavelengths by passing it through a prism. Identifiable as hues or bands of individual colors, most commonly referred to as the colors of a rainbow.

## Split Complementary
Represented by a color and the two colors found on either side of its complement on the color wheel.

## Staccato
Characterized by abrupt and often perceived as violent changes in the visual rhythm as a viewer's eyes move around or through a composition.

## Stippling
An art technique in which clustering small dots or marks creates value.

## Style
The combination of distinctive features of artistic expression, execution, or performance, thought to characterize a particular person, group, school, or era. Also, the way particular artists use media to give their works individuality.

## Subject
An idea or the content represented in an artwork.

## Subjective (art, shapes, color, etc.)
Inventive or creative artwork purely derived from the mind of the artist that reflects a personal viewpoint.

## Subtractive Color
The color sensation produced by the absorption of all other wavelengths except for those reflected back to the viewer.

## Symbolic Shape

When an invented shape communicates ideas or takes on meaning beyond its literal form. Meanings are assigned and agreed upon by the community. Examples include signage and technical diagrams.

## Symbolic Color

When members of a society assign a particular meaning to a color.

## Symmetry

The mirror-like exact duplication and repetition on either side of a central axis.

## Symmetrical Balance

A type of balance created by placing exact objects on either side of a central axis.

## Tactile Texture

The actual surface character of the material either real or manipulated by the artist that a viewer can physically experience.

## Technique

The manner and skill with which an artist employs his tools and materials to achieve an expressive effect.

## Tectonic

A shape possessing the quality of simple massiveness and lacking any significant extrusions or intrusions.

## Tenebrism

A painting technique in which the viewer's attention is focused on important features through the controlled placement of large amounts of dark values close to smaller highly contrasting light areas. Tenebrism exaggerates or emphasizes the effects of chiaroscuro.

## Tension

The visual force of the art elements that affects the balance or counterbalance of a composition.

## Tertiary Color

A color resulting from the mixing of all three primaries in differing amounts or two secondary colors. Tertiary colors are characterized by the neutralization of intensity and hue. They are found on the inner rings on Munsell's color wheel.

## Tessellation

A two-dimensional composition created through the arrangement or repetition of close fitting geometric shapes of distinct colors, with no overlaps and no gaps. From the Latin tessera, meaning a small square piece of stone or tile used for mosaics.

## Texture

The surface character of a material produced by natural forces or through the manipulation of the art elements. Texture can be experience either as a tactile texture (actual texture) or the illusion of touch (visual texture).

## Thematic Unity

A type of unity achieved by assembling similar or related objects, shapes, or forms.

## Three-Dimensional

When an object has or creates the illusion of possessing height, width, and depth.

## Three-Point Perspective

A drawing technique in which vertical lines converge toward a third vanishing point positioned directly above or below the objects.

**Tint**
A color produced by mixing a hue with white.

**Touching**
The close proximity of objects, so that they appear to be attached, even though they are separate objects. In Gestalt theory, touching along with nearness, overlapping, and combining make up the four main types of proximity.

**Tonality**
The dominating hue in a composition, even though other colors may be present.

**Tone**
A low-saturation color produced by mixing a hue with a shade of gray or its complement.

**Transition**
The process of changing from one state or form to another.

**Translation**
A type of symmetry in which the design pattern repeats as though sliding up and down or sideways, without being flipped or turned.

**Transparency**
A visual quality in which an object or art element can be seen clearly through another object or element placed in front of it. In transparency, both forms are seen in their entirety.

**Triadic Color Scheme**
The triadic color scheme uses three colors equally spaced around the color wheel.

**Trompe l'oeil**
A French word that means to "deceive the eye." A painting technique that copies nature with such exactitude that the subject depicted can be mistaken for natural forms. Objects are often in sharp focus and depicted in meticulous detail.

**Two-Dimensional**
Possessing only height or width dimensions.

**Two-Point Perspective**
A system developed to suggest spatial illusion on a two-dimensional plane in which two intersecting parallel lines or planes appear to recede and converge to two vanishing points located on the horizon line.

**Unity**
A sense of oneness created by bringing the art elements together in the appropriate ratio between harmony and variety.

**Value**
The measure of a hue's relative degree of lightness or darkness, as determined by the quantity of light reflected by the color. (Also known as brightness.)

**Value Contrast**
The relationship between adjacent areas of light and dark colors with the highest contrast of all being black and white.

**Value Pattern**
The arrangement or organization of values that controls the compositional movement throughout an artwork and creates a unifying effect.

## Vanishing Point
A point or points positioned on the horizon line, where converging parallel lines appear to meet.

## Variety
Differences introduced to a composition to add individualism and interest. It is achieved through contrast, changing, elaborating, or diversifying art elements on the picture plane. Variety is counterpart to harmony and both contribute to develop a unified composition.

## Vertical Location
A concept used to suggest the illusion of depth on the picture plane. In theory, the further away an object is meant to be, the higher it is placed on the picture plane.

## Vertical Vanishing Point (VVP)
In three-point perspective, the vanishing point at which vertical lines will appear to converge, as determined by the viewer's perspective.

## Vibrating Colors
The physical phenomenon that colors of similar value relationship and strong hue contrast appear to make while abutted to one another.

## Viewing Time
The time a viewer spends exploring an artwork.

## Visual Mixing
An alternative to physically mixing color pigments together, in which pure hues are placed next to one another on the canvas and any and all mixing happens in the eye and the mind of the viewer.

## Visual Movement
The deliberate creation of visual pathways used by the artist to direct the viewer's attention to areas of particular importance within the composition.

## Visual Texture
The illusion of texture created by an artist. (Also referred to as illusion texture.)

## Visual Weight
The relative importance or ability of a visual art element to engage a viewer's attention.

## Volume
A measurable area of defined or occupied space. It is the illusion of enclosed space surrounded by or implied by a shape or form. It also is used to define the space immediately adjacent to and around a painted form. In three-dimensional art, it is the space occupied by the form and or immediate surrounding space. Mass can be thought of as the positive space and volume as the negative space.

## Warm Colors
The subjective temperatures associated with the yellow to red-violet hue segments of the color wheel.

## Worm's Eye View
In a three-point perspective drawing, the exaggerated view from below the horizon line looking up.

# BIBLIOGRAPHY

Agoston, G. A. 1987. *Color theory and its application in art and design*. Berlin, Heidelberg, New York: Springer Verlag.

Albers, J. 1963. *The interaction of color*. New Haven, CT: Yale University Press.

Albers, J. 1975. *Interaction of color*. Rev. ed. New Haven, CT: Yale University Press.

Anderson, D. M. 1961. *Elements of design*. New York: Holt, Rinehart & Winston.

Arnheim, R. 1974. *Art and visual perception: a psychology of the creative eye*. Berkeley: University of California Press.

Battersby, M. 1974. *Trompe-l'oeil: the eye deceived*. New York: St. Martin's Press.

Behrens, R. R. 1984. *Design in the visual arts*. Englewood Cliffs, NJ: Prentice-Hall.

Bevlin, M. E. 1977. *Design through discovery*. 3rd ed. New York: Holt, Rinehart & Winston.

Birren, F. 1961. *Creative color: a dynamic approach for artists and designers*. New York: Van Nostrand Reinhold.

Birren, F. 1961. *Color, form, and space*. New York: Reinhold.

Birren, F., ed. 1969. *Munsell: a grammar of color*. New York: Van Nostrand Reinhold.

Birren, F., ed. 1969. *Ostwald: the color primer*. New York: Van Nostrand Reinhold.

Birren, F. 1970. ed. Itten: *The elements of color*. New York: Van Nostrand Reinhold.

Birren, F. 1987. *Principles of color*. Rev. ed. West Chester, PA: Schiffer Publishing, Limited.

Bloomer, C. M. 1989. *Principles of visual perception*. 2nd ed. New York: Van Nostrand Reinhold.

Bowers, J. 1999. *Introduction to two-dimensional design: understanding form and function*. New York: John Wiley & Sons.

Brusatin, M. 1991. *A history of colors*. Boston and London: Shambala.

Cheathan, F., J. H. Cheathan, and S. A. Haler. 1983. *Design concepts and applications*. Englewood Cliffs, NJ: Prentice-Hall.

Chevreul, M. E. 1967. *The principles of harmony and contrasts of color*. New York: Van Nostrand Reinhold.

Collier, G. 1967. *Form, space and vision*. Englewood Cliffs, NJ: Prentice-Hall.

D'Amelio, J. 1964. *Perspective drawing handbook*. New York: Leon Amiel Publisher.

De Grandis, L. 1987. *Theory and use of color*. New York: Harry N. Abrams.

De Sausmarez, M. 1975. *Basic design: the dynamics of visual form*. New York: Van Nostrand Reinhold.

Diamond, D. G. 1992. *The Bulfinch pocket dictionary of art terms.*. Boston, MA: Bulfinch Press Book; Little, Brown and Company.

Edwards, B. 2004. *Color: a course in mastering the art of mixing colors*. New York. Tarcher/Penguin.

Ehrenzweig, A. 1976. *The hidden order of art: a study in the psychology of artistic imagination*. Berkeley: University of California Press.

Fabri, F. 1967. *Color: a complete guide for artists*. New York: Watson-Guptill.

Feisner, E. A. 2005. *Color studies: how to use color in art and design*. New York: Fairchild Publications; London: Laurence King Publishing.

Gage, J. 2006. *Color in art*. New York: Thames & Hudson.

Gerritsen, F. J. 1974. *Theory and practice of color*. New York: Van Nostrand Reinhold.

Gombrich, E. H. 1961. *Art and illusion: a study in the psychology of pictorial representation*. Princeton, NJ: Princeton University Press.

Hurlburt, A. 1982. *The grid*. New York: Van Nostrand Reinhold.

Itten, J. 1971. *The elements of color*. New York: Van Nostrand Reinhold .

Itten, J. 1976. *Design and form*. 2nd rev. ed. New York: Van Nostrand Reinhold.

Itten, J. 1984. *The art of color*. Rev. ed. New York: Van Nostrand Reinhold.

Kippers, H. 1973. *Color: origin, systems, uses*. New York: Van Nostrand Reinhold.

Myers, J. F. 1989. *The language of visual art*. Orlando, FL: Holt, Rinehart and Winston.

Knobler, N. 1971. *The visual dialogue*. 2nd ed. New York: Holt, Rinehart & Winston.

Kohler, W. 1947. *Gestalt psychology: an introduction to new concepts in modern psychology*. New York: Liveright Publishing Corporation.

Kueppers, H. 1982. *The basic law of color theory*. New York: Barron's Educational Series.

Lauer, D. A. 1979. *Design basics*. Capital City Press, Vermont.

Lauer, D. 1989. *Design basics*. New York: Holt, Rinehart & Winston,.

Lauer, D. A., and S. Pentak, 2006. *Design basics*. 6th ed. Belmont, CA: Wadsworth.

Lindeuer, M. 1989. Aesthetic experience: a neglected topic in the psychology of the arts. In *Psychology and the arts*, ed. O'Hare. Brighton: Harvester Press. pp.307–349.

Lowry, B. 1975. *The visual experience*. 2nd ed. Englewood Cliffs, NJ: Prentice-Hall.

Maier, M. 1977. *Basic principles of design*. New York: Van Nostrand Reinhold.

Munsell, A. 1926. *A color notation*. Baltimore: Munsell Color Company.

Myers, J. F. 1989. *The language of visual art: perception as a basis for design*. Orlando, FL: Holt, Rinehart and Winston.

Newton, I, 1952. *OPTICKS*. Mineola, NY: Dover Publications, Inc.

Ocvirk, O. G., R. E. Stinson, P. R. Wigg, R. O. Bone, and D. L. Cayton. 2013. *Art fundamentals: theory and practice*. 12th ed. New York: McGraw-Hill.

Pentak, S., R. Roth, and D. A. Lauer. 2013. *Design basics: 2D and 3D*. Boston, MA: Wadsworth.

Pink, D. H. 2006. *A whole new mind: why right-brainers will rule the future*. New York: Penguin Group.

Pipes, A. *Introduction to design*. 2009. 2nd ed. Pearson Education Inc., NJ: Pearson Prentice Hall.

Richardson, J. A., F. Coleman, and M. Smith. 1984. *Basic design: systems, elements, applications*. Englewood Cliffs, NJ: Prentice-Hall.

Riley, B. 1995. Color for the painter. In *Color: art and science*, ed. T. Lamb and J. Bourriau. Boston, MA: Cambridge University Press.

Rood, O. 1974. *Modern chromatics*. New York: Van Nostrand Reinhold.

Stern, A. 1984. *How to see color and paint it*. New York: Watson-Guptil Publications.

Stewart, M. 2006. *Launching the imagination: a guide to two-dimensional design*. New York: McGraw-Hill.

Theroux, A. 1994. *The primary colors*. New York: Henry Holt & Co.

Verity, E. 1980. *Color observed*. New York: Van Nostrand Reinhold.

Walters, N. V., and J. Bromham. 1974. *Principles of perspective*. New York: Watson-Guptill Publication.

Weintraub and Walker. 1966. Basic concepts in psychology Series, *Perception*, Brooks/Cole.

Wertheimer, M. 1958. Principles of perceptual organization. In *Readings in perception*, ed. D. C. Beardslee and M. Wertheimer. Princeton: Van Nostrand.

Wong, W. 1972. *Principles of two-dimensional design*. New York: Van Nostrand. Reinhold.

Wong, W. 1997. *Principles of two-dimensional design*. New York: John Wiley & Sons.

Zelanski, P., and M. P. Fisher. 1984. *Design principles and problems*. New York: CBS College Publishing.

Zelanski, P., and M. P. Fisher. 2007. *Shaping space*. Belmont CA: Thompson Wadsworth.

## WEB REFERENCES

Causes of color: webexhibits.org/causesofcolorfindex.html

Color matters: www.colormatters.com

Munsell color system: www.applepainter.com

Pigments through the ages: webexhibits.org/pigments/index.html

Virtual color museum: www.colorsystem.com

Fibonacci numbers and the golden section: www.goldenmeangauge.co.ukjfibonacci.htm www.mcs.surrey.ac.uk/PersonaljR.Knott/ Fibonaccijfib.html